# Level B
# Contents

**BASIC** Phonics Skills

©2004 by Evan-Moor Corp. • Basic Phonics Skills, Level B • EMC 3319

# Basic Phonics Skills
## What's in Level B?

## Reproducible Skill Sheets

Choose from a number of reproducibles to practice each skill.
Skill sheets present varying levels of difficulty to meet individual student needs.

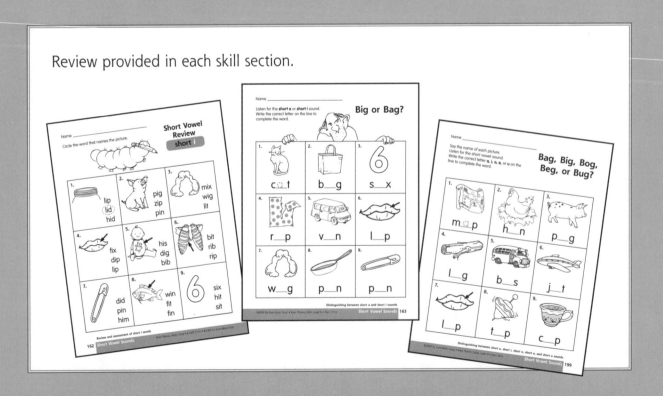

easiest ⟵⟶ more difficult

Review provided in each skill section.

# Word Family Sliders and Skill Sheets

Word Family Sliders provide repeat practice of major word families.

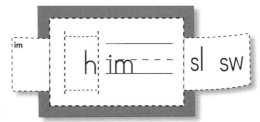

Activity sheets reinforce word families presented on the sliders.

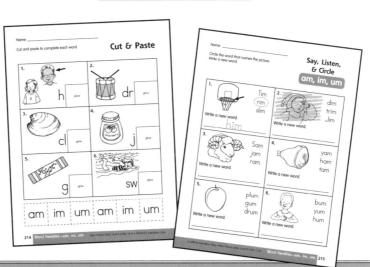

# Little Phonics Readers

10 short vowel readers

10 word family readers

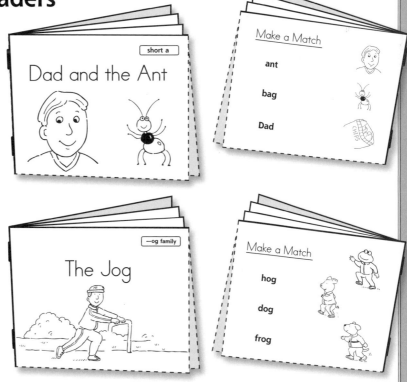

# Tracking Student Progress

Use the form on page 5 to record the progress of each student. The rubric provided below will help you assess each student's level of competence. Students who fail to achieve a 2 or 3 level should be provided additional instruction and practice until they become proficient.

| Mastered **3** | • The student is able to complete the activity independently.<br>• The student is able to complete the activity correctly.<br>• The student is able to answer questions about the phonetic principle being practiced. |
|---|---|
| Showed Adequate Understanding **2** | • The student is able to complete the activity with little assistance.<br>• The student is able to complete the activity with minimal errors.<br>• The student is able to answer some questions about the phonetic principle being practiced. |
| Showed Inconsistent Understanding **1** | • The student required assistance to complete the activity.<br>• The student made several errors.<br>• The student did not appear to understand the phonetic principle being practiced. |
| Showed Little or No Understanding **0** | • The student required one-to-one assistance to complete the activity, or was unable to complete the activity.<br>• The student made many errors.<br>• The student showed no understanding of the phonetic principle being practiced. |

Basic Phonics Skills, Level B • EMC 3319 • ©2004 by Evan-Moor Corp.

Name _____

# Basic Phonics Skills, Level B
## Student Record Form

| Sound or Skill Practiced | Level B Page Number | Date Completed | 3 Mastered | 2 Showed Adequate Understanding | 1 Showed Inconsistent Understanding | 0 Showed Little or No Understanding |
|---|---|---|---|---|---|---|
| | | | | | | |
| | | | | | | |
| | | | | | | |
| | | | | | | |
| | | | | | | |
| | | | | | | |
| | | | | | | |
| | | | | | | |
| | | | | | | |
| | | | | | | |
| | | | | | | |
| | | | | | | |
| | | | | | | |

# The Benefits of Phonics Instruction

Words are made of letters, and letters stand for sounds. That is the simple basis for providing phonics instruction to all beginning readers. Research has shown that all children will benefit from being taught the sound-spelling connection of the English language (Chall, 1967). Phonics instruction leads to decoding, which gives beginning readers one more strategy to use when faced with an unfamiliar word.

## Research has shown the following to be true:

- Strong decoding skills in early readers correlate highly with future success in reading comprehension (Beck and Juel, 1995).
- As more and more "sounded-out" words become sight words, readers have more time to devote to the real reason for reading: making meaning from print (LaBerge and Samuels, 1974; Freedman and Calfee, 1984).
- Readers who are good decoders read more words than those who are poor decoders (Juel, 1988).
- Children with limited learning opportunities and abilities benefit most from phonics instruction, but more able children also benefit (Chall, 1967).
- Those who are successful decoders do not depend on context clues as much as those who are poor decoders (Gough and Juel, 1991).

The best readers can decode words. As a result, those readers grow in word recognition, fluency, automaticity, and comprehension. "Sounding out" unfamiliar words is a skill that benefits all readers. These new words quickly become "sight words," those recognized immediately in text, which allow the reader to spend more time on new words. This cycle is the foundation that creates reading success, and successful readers are better learners.

# BASIC Phonics Skills

Basic Phonics Skills, Level B • EMC 3319 • ©2004 by Evan-Moor Corp.

# Beginning and Ending Consonant Sounds

Name _____

Circle the picture if you hear the /b/ sound at the beginning.

## Bb
**b**ig
**b**alloon

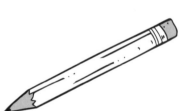

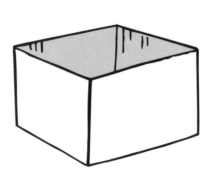

**To the Teacher:** Review the picture names with students.
(dog, bee, box, pencil, barn)

**Recognizing the beginning /b/ sound**

**Beginning and Ending**
**Consonant Sounds**

Name _____

Say the name of each picture.
Draw a line to the bucket if the word begins
with the /b/ sound.
Write the letter **b** if you hear it.

# In the Bucket

___ook

___ug

___oll

**b**ucket

___ell

___one

Name _____

Cut out the pictures.
Glue the picture in a box if the word ends
with the /b/ sound.

# Rub-a-Dub-Tub

tub

glue          glue          glue

**Recognizing the ending /b/ sound**

**Beginning and Ending**
**Consonant Sounds**                    Basic Phonics Skills, Level B • EMC 3319 • ©2004 by Evan-Moor Corp.

Name _____

Write the letter **b** in the box if the word ends
with the /b/ sound.

# At the End

| | |
|---|---|
| **1.** su b | **2.** be ☐ |
| **3.** mo ☐ | **4.** ri ☐ |
| **5.** cri ☐ | **6.** tu ☐ |

**Recognizing the ending /b/ sound**

Beginning and Ending
**Consonant Sounds**   11

Name _____

Say the name of each picture.
Listen for the /b/ sound.
Do you hear it at the beginning or the end?
Write the letter **b** in the correct box.

# Beginning or Ending b?

1.

2.

3.

4.

5.

6.

7.

8.

**Distinguishing between the beginning and ending /b/ sound**

**Beginning and Ending Consonant Sounds**

Basic Phonics Skills, Level B • EMC 3319 • ©2004 by Evan-Moor Corp.

Name _____

Say the name of the picture.
Fill in the circle to show where you hear
the /b/ sound. Write the letter **b** on the line.

# Begins or Ends with b?

| | |
|---|---|
| **1.**  | ● ___us  ○ su___ |
| **2.**  | ○ la___  ○ ___at |
| **3.**  | ○ ___ug  ○ tu___ |
| **4.**  | ○ ___ug  ○ jo___ |
| **5.**  | ○ cra___  ○ ___at |
| **6.**  | ○ ___ib  ○ bi___ |

Completing words with the /b/ sound

Name _____

Circle the picture if you hear the /s/ sound at the beginning.

Ss
sub

**To the Teacher:** Review the picture names with students.
(seal, soup, sandwich, pizza, salt, bear)

**Recognizing the beginning /s/ sound**

Name _____

Say the name of each picture.
Draw a line to the sack if you hear the /s/ sound
at the beginning.
Write the letter **s** if you hear it.

# Such a Snack

___oap

___eal

___ock

**s**ack

___un

___ar

___ix

Name _____

Cut out the pictures.
Glue the picture in a box if the word ends
with the /s/ sound.

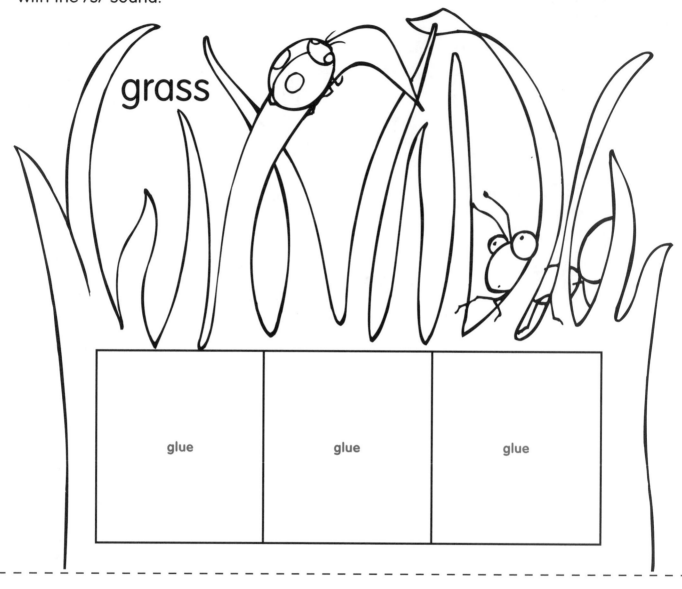

grass

| glue | glue | glue |

**Recognizing the ending /s/ sound**

**Beginning and Ending
Consonant Sounds**

Basic Phonics Skills, Level B • EMC 3319 • ©2004 by Evan-Moor Corp.

Name _____

Write the letter **s** if the name of the picture ends with the /s/ sound.

# The End

| | | |
|---|---|---|
| 1. 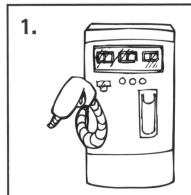 ga s__ | 2.  bu___ | 3.  bu___ |
| 4.  ye___ | 5.  su___ | 6.  do___ |

Adding the ending /s/ sound (spelled s)

Name _____

Sometimes a double **ss** stands for the /s/ sound. Write the letters **ss** if the picture name ends with the /s/ sound.

# Seeing Double

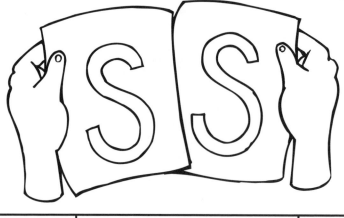

| | | |
|---|---|---|
| 1.  dre S S | 2.  gra ___ ___ | 3.  ki ___ ___ |
| 4.  do ___ ___ | 5. 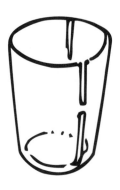 gla ___ ___ | 6.  fi ___ ___ |

Adding the ending /s/ sound (spelled ss)

**Beginning and Ending Consonant Sounds**                     Basic Phonics Skills, Level B • EMC 3319 • ©2004 by Evan-Moor Corp.

Name _____

Cut out the pictures. Glue the picture by
the sub if it begins with the /s/ sound.
Glue the picture by the bus if it ends with the /s/ sound.

# Sub or Bus?

sub

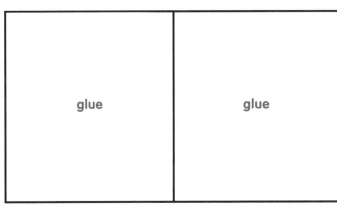

glue    glue

bus

glue    glue

**Distinguishing between the beginning and ending /s/ sound**

Name _____

Write the letter(s) **s** or **ss** on the lines where you hear the /s/ sound.

# Something Silly

The octopus has a glass.

1. __s__un

2. ___ub

3. gra___ ___

4. ___oup

5. ___aw

6. dre___ ___

**Completing words with the /s/ sound**

**Beginning and Ending Consonant Sounds**

Basic Phonics Skills, Level B • EMC 3319 • ©2004 by Evan-Moor Corp.

Name _____

Circle the picture if the name begins with the /m/ sound.

# Listen for m

Mm
**m**y
**m**onkey

MILK

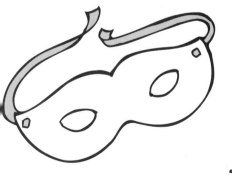

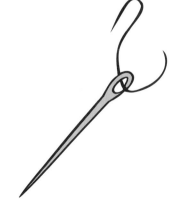

**To the Teacher:** Review the picture names with students.
(banana, milk, moon, mask, mouse, needle)

**Recognizing the beginning /m/ sound**

**Beginning and Ending
Consonant Sounds**

Name _____

Write the letter **m** if the name of the picture begins with the /m/ sound.

# Miss Mouse

| 1. | 2. | 3. |
|---|---|---|
|  | 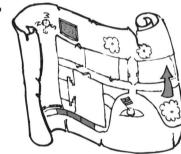 | |
| m̲an | ___ap | ___est |
| 4. | 5. | 6. |
|  |  |  |
| ___op | ___oon | ___ug |

Adding the beginning /m/ sound

**Beginning and Ending**
**Consonant Sounds**          Basic Phonics Skills, Level B • EMC 3319 • ©2004 by Evan-Moor Corp.

Name _____

Circle the objects in Sam's room if their names end with the /m/ sound.

# Sam's Room

**Beginning and Ending
Consonant Sounds**   **23**

Name _____

Write the letter **m** if you hear the /m/ sound at the end.

ra**m**

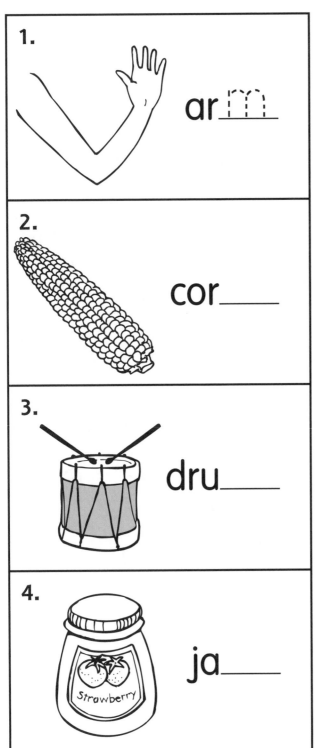

1.

ar _m_

2.

cor___

3.

dru___

4.

ja___

5.

plu___

6.

bu___

7.

ha___

8.

far___

Adding the ending /m/ sound

Name _____

Say the name of each picture.
Listen for the /m/ sound. Do you hear it
at the beginning or at the end?
Write the letter **m** in the correct box.

# Beginning or Ending m?

## moon

## drum

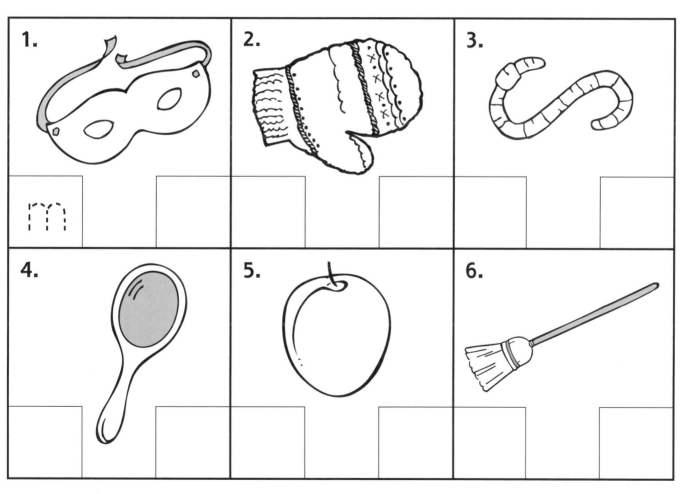

1.

2.

3.

m

4.

5.

6.

**Distinguishing between the beginning and ending /m/ sound**

Name _____

Say the name of the picture.
Write the letter **m** on the line where you hear
the /m/ sound.

# Mom

| | | |
|---|---|---|
| **1.**  <br> m̲oon___ | **2.**  <br> ___ug___ | **3.** 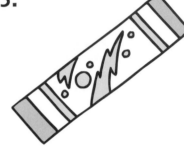 <br> ___gu___ |
| **4.**  <br> ___cla___ | **5.** 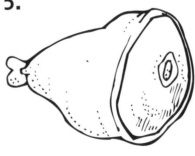 <br> ___ha___ | **6.**  <br> ___dru___ |

Completing words with the /m/ sound

Basic Phonics Skills, Level B • EMC 3319 • ©2004 by Evan-Moor Corp.

Name _____

Say the name of each picture.
Listen for the beginning sound.
Draw a circle around the letter that stands for
the beginning sound.

1.

b    s    (m)

2.

b    s    m

3.

b    s    m

4.

b    s    m

5.

b    s    m

6.

b    s    m

7.

b    s    m

8.

b    s    m

9.

b    s    m

Reviewing beginning sounds /b/ /s/ /m/

Name _____

Say the name of each picture.
Listen for the beginning sound.
Write the letter that stands for the beginning sound.

1. m

2.

3.

4.

5.

6.

7.

8.

9.

**Reviewing beginning sounds /b/ /s/ /m/**

**Beginning and Ending**
**Consonant Sounds**                    Basic Phonics Skills, Level B • EMC 3319 • ©2004 by Evan-Moor Corp

Name _____

Say the name of each picture.
Listen for the ending sound.
Draw a circle around the letter that stands for the ending sound.

| 1. | 2. | 3. |
|---|---|---|
| b  s  (m) | b  s  m | b  s  m |

| 4. | 5. | 6. |
|---|---|---|
| b  s  m | b  s  m | b  s  m |

| 7. | 8. | 9. |
|---|---|---|
| b  s  m | b  s  m | b  s  m |

Reviewing ending sounds /b/ /s/ /m/

Name _____

Say the name of each picture.
Listen for the ending sound.
Write the letter that stands for the ending sound.

1. m

2.

3.

4.

5.

6.

7.

8.

9.

Reviewing ending sounds /b/ /s/ /m/

Name _____

Circle the picture if you hear the /t/ sound at the beginning.

# Listen for t

**Tt**
tent

**To the Teacher:** Review the picture names with students.
(turkey, cat, two, telephone, tire, desk)

Recognizing the beginning /t/ sound

Name _____

Say the name of each picture.
Listen for the beginning sound.
Write the letter **t** if you hear it.

# Turtle Tim

| | | |
|---|---|---|
| 1. 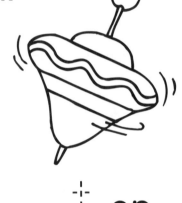  __t_op | 2. 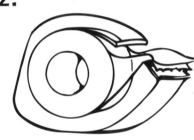  ___ape | 3.   ___en |
| 4.   ___ime | 5. 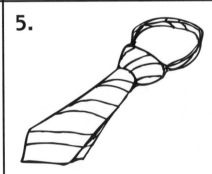  ___ie | 6. 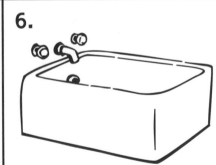  ___ub |

**Adding the beginning /t/ sound**

Name _____

Say the name of each picture.
Draw a line to the boat if the word ends
with the /t/ sound.

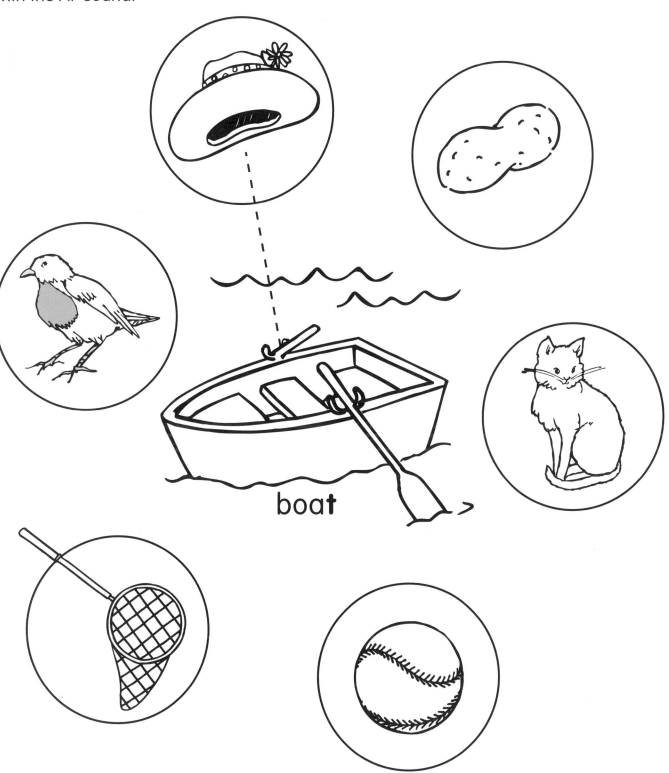

boat

Name _____

Say the name of each picture.
Write the letter **t** if the name ends with the /t/ sound.

# What Do You Hear?

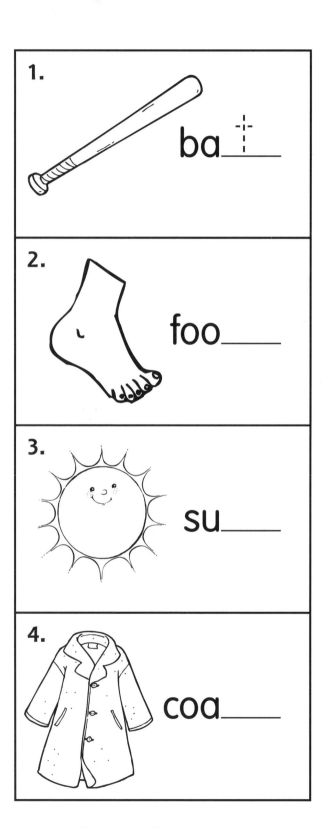

1. ba_t_

2. foo____

3. su____

4. coa____

5. boo____

6. ha____

7. moo____

8. ca____

**Adding the ending /t/ sound**

**Beginning and Ending
Consonant Sounds**

Basic Phonics Skills, Level B • EMC 3319 • ©2004 by Evan-Moor Corp.

Name _____

Say the name of each picture. Listen for the /t/ sound.
Do you hear it at the beginning or the end?
Write the letter **t** in the correct box.

# Beginning or Ending t?

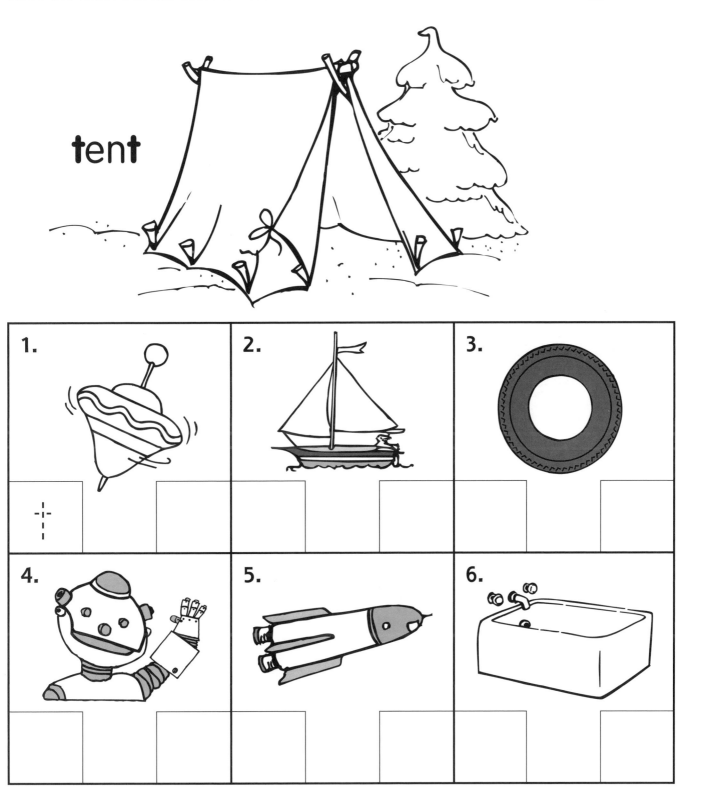

tent

| 1. | 2. | 3. |
| 4. | 5. | 6. |

**Distinguishing between the beginning and ending /t/ sound**

Name _____

Say the name of each picture.
Where do you hear the /t/ sound?
Write the letter **t** at the beginning or the end of the word.

# Listen for the Sound

| | | |
|---|---|---|
| **1.** 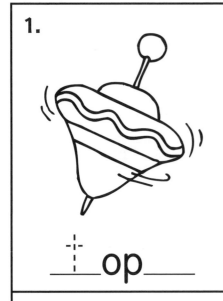 __†__op____ | **2.**  ____boa____ | **3.**  ____ca____ |
| **4.** 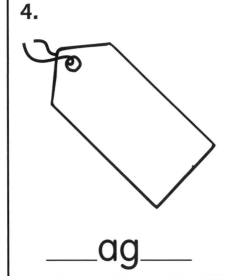 ____ag____ | **5.** 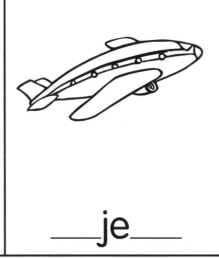 ____je____ | **6.**  ____goa____ |

**Completing words with the /t/ sound**

Beginning and Ending
**Consonant Sounds**
Basic Phonics Skills, Level B • EMC 3319 • ©2004 by Evan-Moor Corp.

Name _____

Circle the picture if you hear the /f/ sound at the beginning.

# F f
**f**ive
**f**lowers

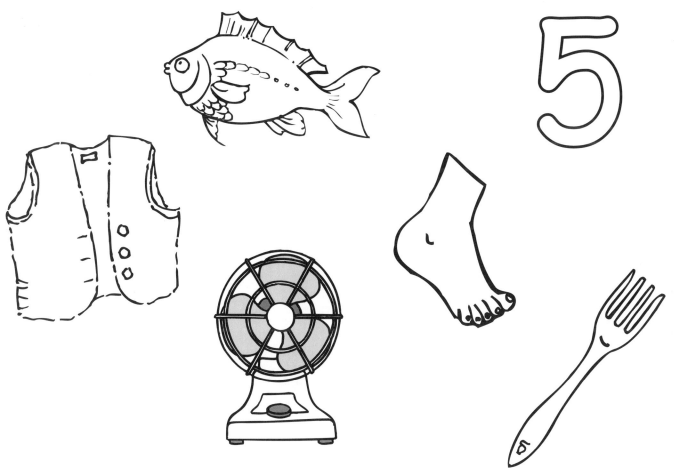

**To the Teacher:** Review the picture names with students.
(fish, five, vest, fan, foot, fork)

**Recognizing the beginning /f/ sound**

Name _____

Say the name of each picture.
Write the letter **f** in the blank to make a new word.
Draw a line to the picture that goes with the new word.

# Switch to f

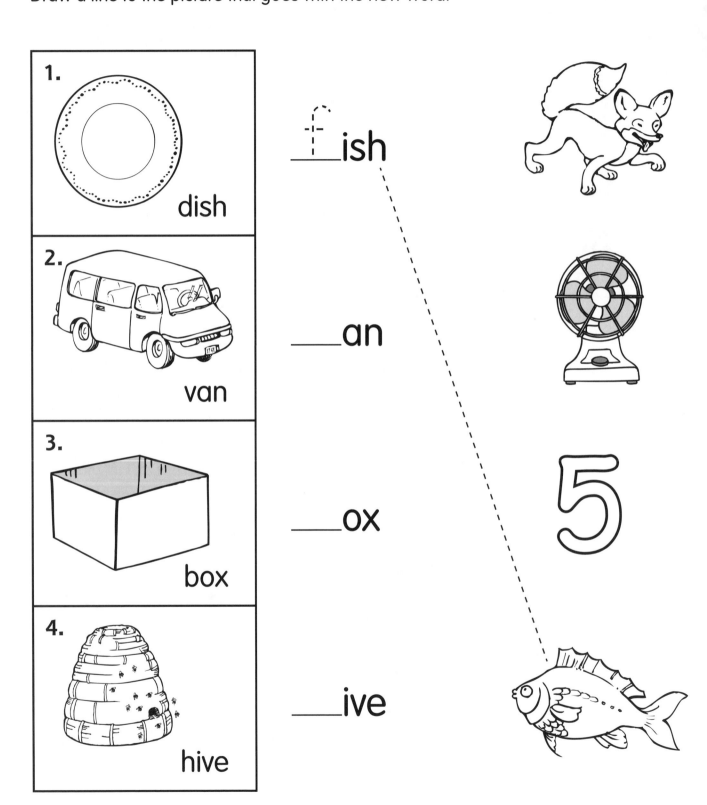

1. dish

2. van

3. box

4. hive

___ish

___an

___ox

___ive

Adding the beginning /f/ sound

Basic Phonics Skills, Level B • EMC 3319 • ©2004 by Evan-Moor Corp.

Name _____

Cut out the pictures.
Glue the picture in a box if the word ends with
the /f/ sound.

# Falling Leaf

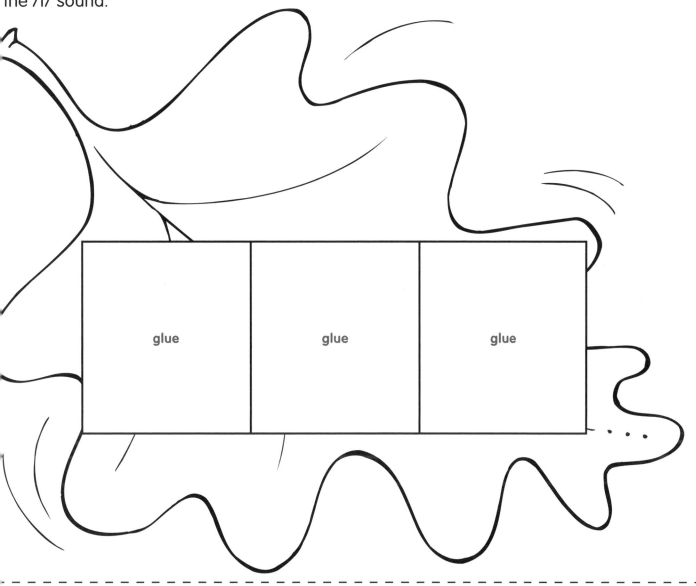

| glue | glue | glue |

Name _____

Say the name of each picture.
Write the letter **f** at the end of each word
if its name ends with the /f/ sound.

**Woof!**
**Woof!**

woof!

| | | |
|---|---|---|
| 1.  wol_f_ | 2.  lea____ | 3.  boo____ |
| 4. 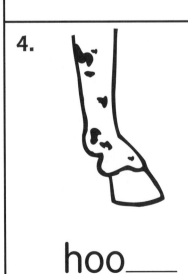 hoo____ | 5.  el____ | 6. 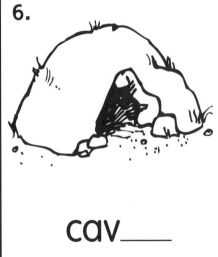 cav____ |

**Adding the ending /f/ sound**

Beginning and Ending
**Consonant Sounds**

Basic Phonics Skills, Level B • EMC 3319 • ©2004 by Evan-Moor Corp.

Name _____

Write the letters **ff** on the lines if the picture name ends with the /f/ sound.

# Jeff's Stuff

In some words, the double **ff** stands for the /f/ sound.

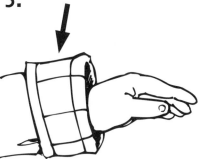

| 1. | 2. | 3. |
|---|---|---|
|  o f f |  hi____ ____ | cu____ ____ |

| 4. | 5. | 6. |
|---|---|---|
|  cli____ ____ |  glo____ ____ |  pu____ ____ |

**Adding the ending /f/ sound (spelled ff)**

Name _____

Draw a line to the fox if the name begins with
the /f/ sound.
Draw a line to the wolf if the name ends with
the /f/ sound.

fox

wolf

**Distinguishing between the beginning and ending /f/ sound**

Name _____

Write the letter **f** at the beginning or end of the word to show where you hear the /f/ sound. Draw a line to connect the pictures that fit with each other.

# Find the Fit

**1.**

__f__ork____

____ootball____

**2.**

____oot____

____ox____

**3.**

____wol____

____che____

Name _____

Circle the picture if you hear the /k/ sound at the beginning.

# Listen for k

Kk
kite

**To the Teacher:** Review the picture names with students.
(tooth, kangaroo, kitten, sock, king, key)

**Recognizing the beginning /k/ sound (spelled k)**

Basic Phonics Skills, Level B • EMC 3319 • ©2004 by Evan-Moor Corp.

Name _____

Say the name of each picture.
Write the beginning sound.

## Cute Kangaroo

**c** and **k** make the same sound

| 1. | 2. | 3. |
|---|---|---|
| ☐at | ☐ey | ☐ite |

| 4. | 5. | 6. |
|---|---|---|
| ☐ow | ☐ing | ☐oat |

**Recognizing the beginning /k/ sound (spelled c or k )**

Beginning and Ending
**Consonant Sounds**      **45**

Name _____

Glue the pictures onto the wall if their
name ends with the /k/ sound.

Look!

look

glue          glue

glue          glue

**Recognizing the ending /k/ sound (spelled k or ck)**

Basic Phonics Skills, Level B • EMC 3319 • ©2004 by Evan-Moor Corp.

Name _____

Draw a line to the key if the picture name begins
with the /k/ sound.
Draw a line to the sack if the picture name ends
with the /k/ sound.

# Where Is It?

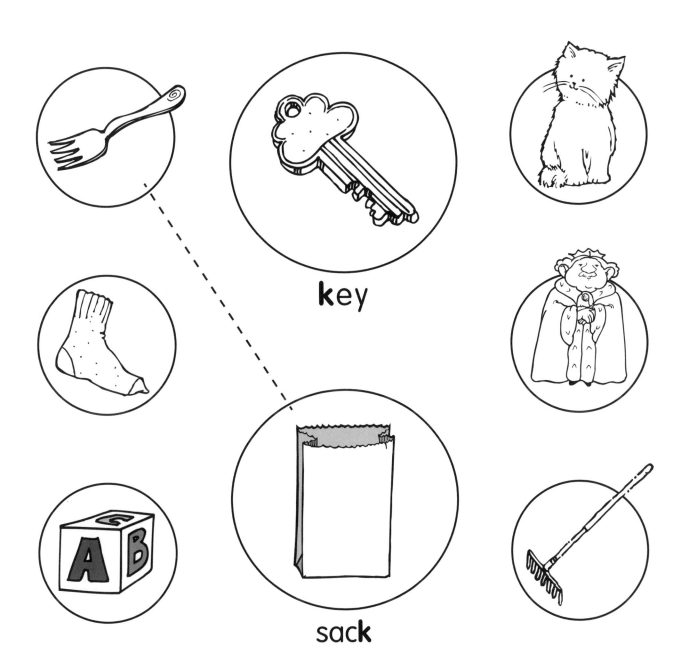

key

sack

Distinguishing between the beginning and ending /k/ sound

Beginning and Ending
**Consonant Sounds**    **47**

Name _____

Say the name of each picture.
Listen to the ending sound.
Write the letter(s) **k** or **ck**.

 **At the End**

1. clo_c k_

2. des___

3. sti___ ___

4. boo___

5. so___

6. sa___

7. hoo___

8. lo___ ___

Adding the ending /k/ sound (spelled k or ck)

 Beginning and Ending
**Consonant Sounds**                      Basic Phonics Skills, Level B • EMC 3319 • ©2004 by Evan-Moor Corp.

Name _____

Say the name of each object.
Write the correct letter(s) **k** or **ck** in the boxes.

# Spell It

1. k ing

2. sti ☐ ☐

3. lo ☐ ☐

4. ☐ ite

5. ☐ itten

6. so ☐ ☐

7. du ☐ ☐

8. boo ☐

9. hoo ☐

**Completing words with the /k/ sound (spelled k or ck)**

Name _____

Say the name of each picture.
Listen for the beginning sound.
Draw a circle around the letter that stands for
the beginning sound.

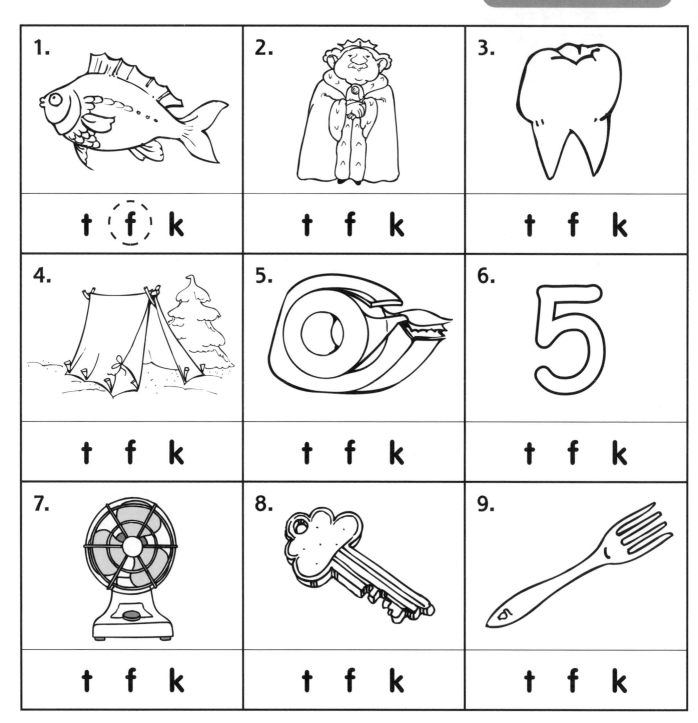

1. t (f) k

2. t f k

3. t f k

4. t f k

5. t f k

6. t f k

7. t f k

8. t f k

9. t f k

**Reviewing beginning sounds /t/ /f/ /k/**

Name _____

Say the name of each picture.
Listen for the beginning sound.
Write the letter that stands for the beginning sound.

# More Review
# Beginning
# Sounds

## t f k

| | | |
|---|---|---|
| 1. k | 2. | 3. |
| 4. | 5. | 6. |
| 7. | 8. | 9. |

Name _____

Say the name of each picture.
Listen for the ending sound.
Draw a circle around the letter that stands for
the ending sound.

| 1. | 2. | 3. |
|---|---|---|
| t f (k) | t f k | t f k |

| 4. | 5. | 6. |
|---|---|---|
| t f k | t f k | t f k |

| 7. | 8. | 9. |
|---|---|---|
| t f k | t f k | t f k |

Reviewing ending sounds /t/ /f/ /k/

Name _____

Say the name of each picture.
Listen for the ending sound.
Write the letter that stands for the ending sound.

1.      k

2.

3.

4.

5.

6.

7.

8.

9.

Reviewing ending sounds /t/ /f/ /k/

Name _____

Color the picture purple if the picture name begins like **pocket**.

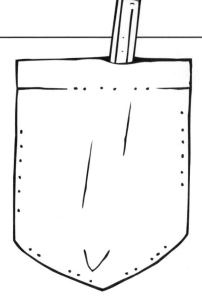

## Pp
**p**encil
**p**ocket

**To the Teacher:** Review the picture names with students.
(pan, pillow, cat, pencil, pig, popcorn)

**Recognizing the beginning /p/ sound**

Basic Phonics Skills, Level B • EMC 3319 • ©2004 by Evan-Moor Corp.

Name _____

Write the letter **p** at the beginning of the word if it begins like **pail**.

# Pat's Pail

| 1. | 2. | 3. |
|---|---|---|
| <u>p</u>in | ___up | ___ie |
| 4. | 5. | 6. |
| ___ar | ___ig | ___ear |

**Adding the beginning /p/ sound**

Name _____

If the name begins with the /p/ sound,
draw a line to the pig.

If the name ends with the /p/ sound,
draw a line to the sheep.

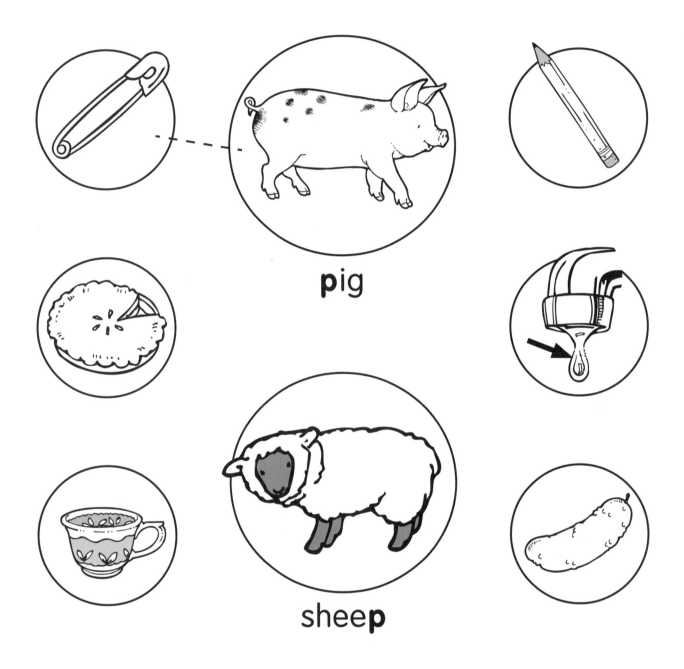

**p**ig

shee**p**

Recognizing the beginning and ending /p/ sound

**Beginning and Ending
Consonant Sounds**      Basic Phonics Skills, Level B • EMC 3319 • ©2004 by Evan-Moor Corp.

Name _____

Write the letter **p** if the picture name ends with the /p/ sound.

# Hop, Hop, Hop

| 1.  | 2.  | 3.  |
|---|---|---|
| ca_p_ | jee___ | su___ |
| 4.  | 5.  | 6. 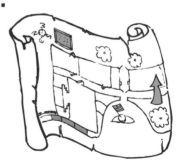 |
| shee___ | tu___ | ma___ |

Adding the ending **/p/** sound

Name _____

Say the name of each picture. Where do you hear the /p/ sound? Fill in the circle to show if the **p** is at the beginning or the end.

# Pick a Place

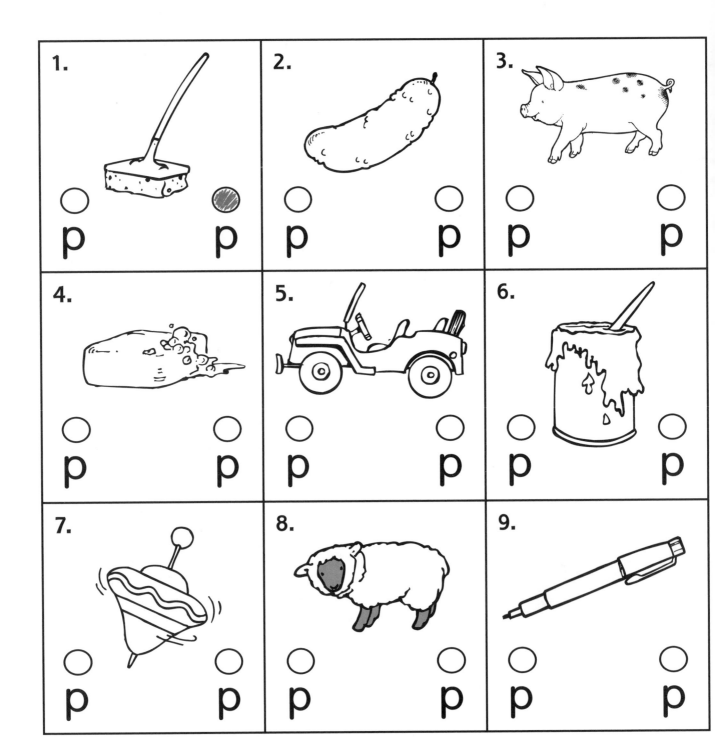

Distinguishing between the beginning and ending /p/ sound

**Beginning and Ending Consonant Sounds**

Basic Phonics Skills, Level B • EMC 3319 • ©2004 by Evan-Moor Corp.

Name _____

Say the name of each picture.
Write the letter **p** where
you hear the /p/ sound.

# Jump, Pet!

1.

__p_ot___

2.

___ma___

3.

___ig___

4.

___up___

5.

___ail___

6.

___to___

Completing words with the /p/ sound

Name _____

Circle the picture if the name begins with the /r/ sound.

Rr
red
roses

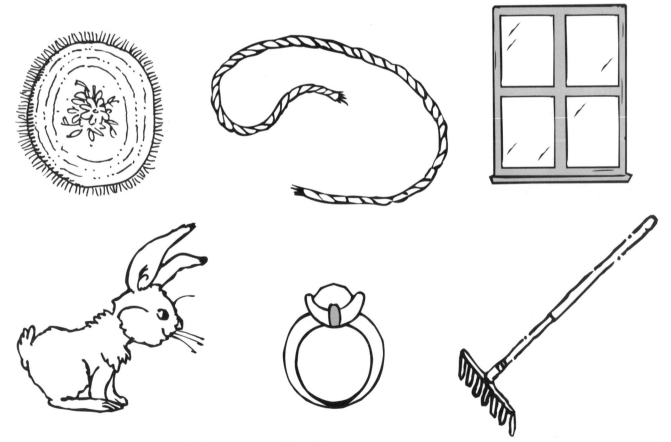

**To the Teacher:** Review the picture names with students.
(rug, rope, window, rabbit, ring, rake)

**Recognizing the beginning /r/ sound**

**60**

Name _____

Write the letter **r** on the line if the picture name begins with the /r/ sound.

| 1. | 2. | 3. |
|---|---|---|
| r | | ___ |
| | ___ | ___ |

| 4. | 5. | 6. |
|---|---|---|
| ___ | ___ | ___ |

**Adding the beginning /r/ sound**

Name _____

Color the star if the picture name ends with the /r/ sound.

# A Far, Far Star

Little star, big star,
Near star, far star.
My star, your star, our star!

Name _____

Write the letter **r** on the line if the picture name ends with the /r/ sound.

# In the Jar

| 1. | 2. | 3. |
|---|---|---|

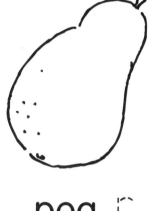

pea_r_

dee____

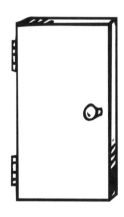

doo____

| 4. | 5. | 6. |
|---|---|---|

bel____

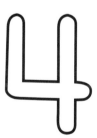

fou____

ca____

Adding the /r/ sound

Name _____

Cut out the pictures. Glue them by the rug if their name begins with the /r/ sound.
Glue them by the chair if their name ends with the /r/ sound.

# Rug or Chair?

rug

| | |
|---|---|
| glue | glue |
| glue | glue |

chair

| | |
|---|---|
| glue | glue |
| glue | glue |

**Distinguishing between the beginning and ending /r/ sound**

**Beginning and Ending Consonant Sounds**    Basic Phonics Skills, Level B • EMC 3319 • ©2004 by Evan-Moor Corp.

Name _____

Write the letter **r** on the lines where you hear the /r/ sound.

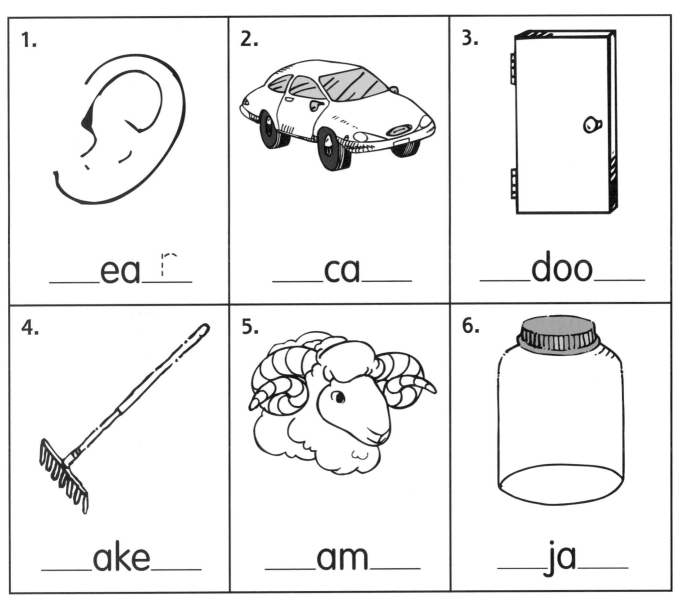

1. ___ea___

2. ___ca___

3. ___doo___

4. ___ake___

5. ___am___

6. ___ja___

**Completing words with the /r/ sound**

Name _____

Circle the picture if the name begins with the /v/ sound.

# Vera's Vest

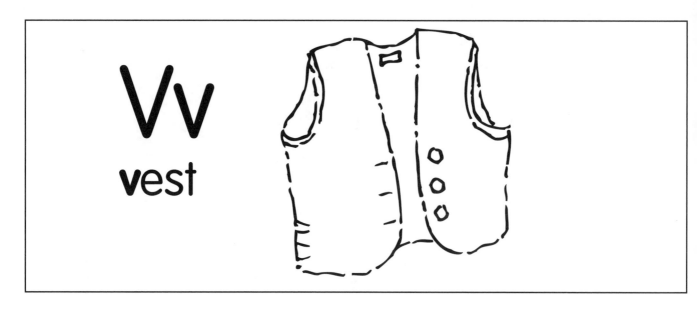

**Vv**
vest

**To the Teacher:** Review the picture names with students.
(vine, vase, violin, chair, fish, van)

**Recognizing the beginning /v/ sound**

Name _____

Write the letter **v** on the line if the word begins with the /v/ sound.

__v__ an

___est

___ig

___ase

___ine

___an

Adding the beginning /v/ sound

©2004 by Evan-Moor Corp. • Basic Phonics Skills, Level B • EMC 3319

Name _____

Cut out the pictures. Glue them by the vase if their name begins with the /v/ sound. Glue them by the glove if their name ends with the /v/ sound.

# First or Last?

vase

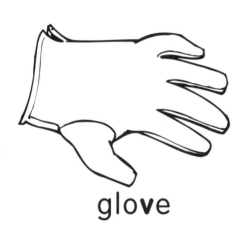

glove

| glue | glue |
|------|------|
| glue | glue |

| glue | glue |
|------|------|
| glue | glue |

**Recognizing the ending /v/ sound**

**Beginning and Ending Consonant Sounds**

Basic Phonics Skills, Level B • EMC 3319 • ©2004 by Evan-Moor Corp.

Name _____

If the name begins with the /v/ sound,
draw a line to the valley.

If the name ends with the /v/ sound,
draw a line to the cave.

# Valley or Cave?

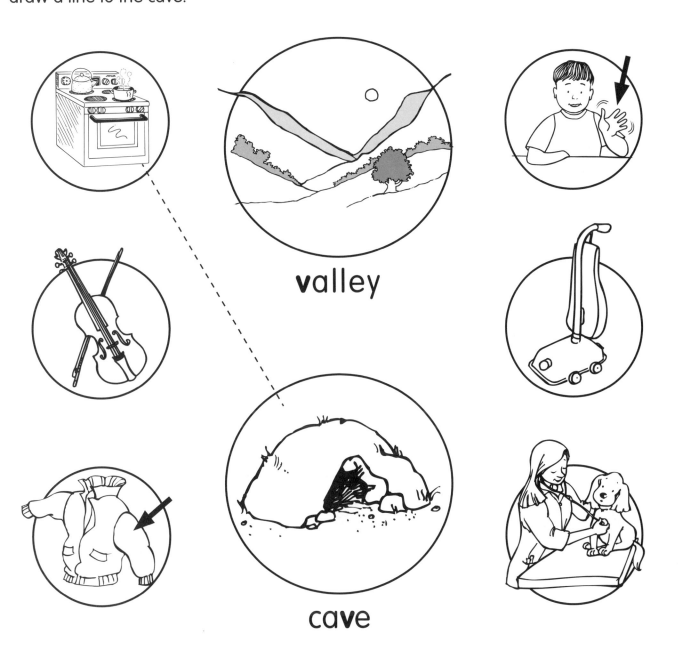

valley

cave

Name _____

Say the name of each picture. Where do you hear the /v/ sound? Fill in the circle to show if the **v** is at the beginning or the end.

# Val's Vacation

1.

○ V    ○ V

2.

○ V    ○ V

3.

○ V    ○ V

4.

○ V    ○ V

5.

○ V    ○ V

6.

○ V    ○ V

**Completing words with the /v/ sound**

**Beginning and Ending Consonant Sounds**

Basic Phonics Skills, Level B • EMC 3319 • ©2004 by Evan-Moor Corp.

Name _____

Say the name of each picture.
Listen for the beginning sound.
Draw a circle around the letter that stands for
the beginning sound.

p r v

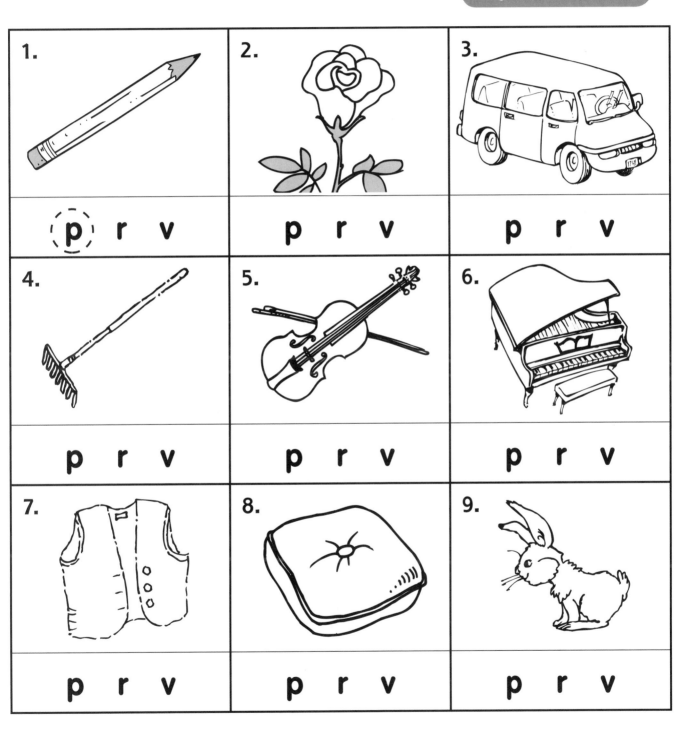

1. (p) r v

2. p r v

3. p r v

4. p r v

5. p r v

6. p r v

7. p r v

8. p r v

9. p r v

**Reviewing the beginning sounds /p/ /r/ /v/**

Name _____

Say the name of each picture.
Listen for the beginning sound.
Write the letter that stands for the beginning sound.

1. P

2.

3. Be Mine

4.

5.

6.

7.

8.

9.

**Reviewing the beginning sounds /p/ /r/ /v/**

Beginning and Ending
**Consonant Sounds**    Basic Phonics Skills, Level B • EMC 3319 • ©2004 by Evan-Moor Corp.

Name _____

Say the name of each picture.
Listen for the ending sound.
Draw a circle around the letter that stands for
the ending sound.

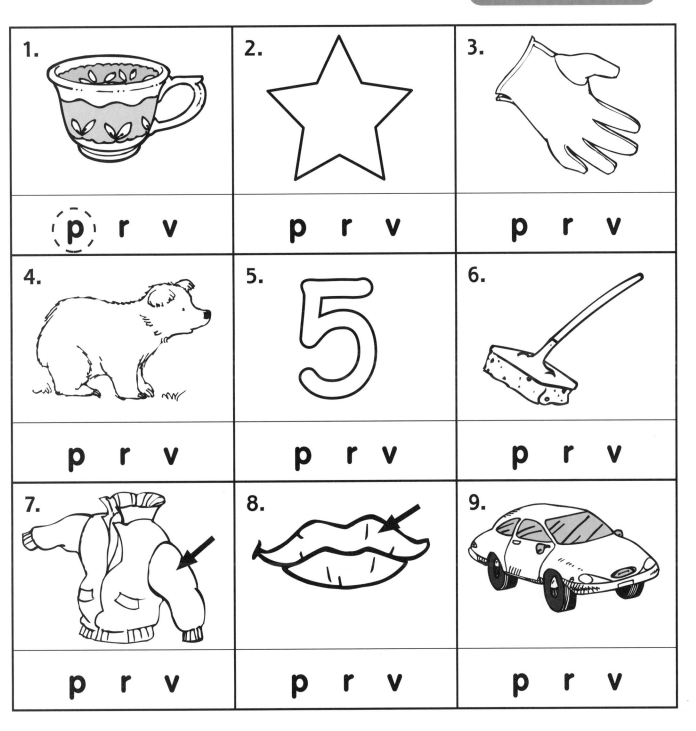

1. p r v

2. p r v

3. p r v

4. p r v

5. p r v

6. p r v

7. p r v

8. p r v

9. p r v

Reviewing the ending sounds /p/ /r/ /v/

Name _____

Say the name of each picture.
Listen for the ending sound.
Write the letter that stands for the ending sound.

1.

2.

3.

4.

5.

6.

7.

8.

9.

10.

11.

12.

**Reviewing the ending sounds /p/ /r/ /v/**

Name _____

Circle the picture if you hear the /d/ sound at the beginning.

# Dig, Dog, Dig!

Dd

**d**ig

**d**og

**To the Teacher:** Review the picture names with students.
(doll, dinosaur, dollar, ball, toothbrush, duck)

Recognizing the beginning /d/ sound

Name _____

Write the letter **d** if the name begins like **duck**.

# The Duck

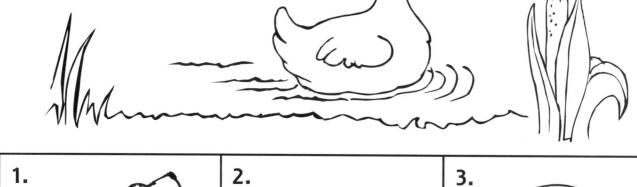

| | | |
|---|---|---|
| 1. <br> d__og | 2. <br> __ear | 3. <br> __ime |
| 4. <br> __esk | 5. <br> __en | 6. <br> __ish |

**Adding the beginning /d/ sound**

Basic Phonics Skills, Level B • EMC 3319 • ©2004 by Evan-Moor Corp.

Name _____

Color the bead red if the object's name ends with
the /d/ sound.

# A Red Bead

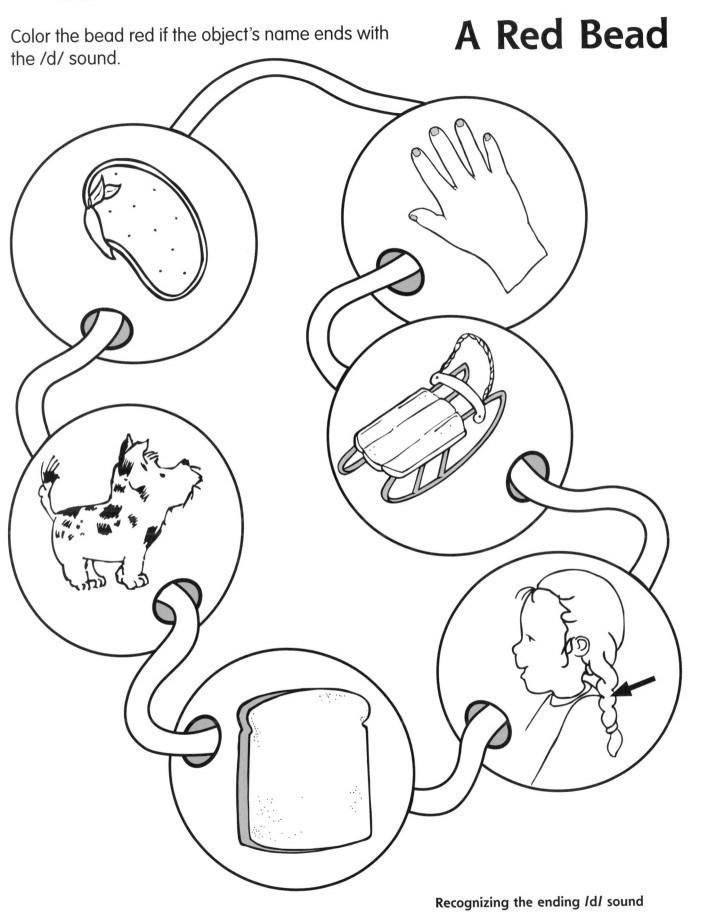

Recognizing the ending /d/ sound

Name _____

Write the letter **d** if the picture name ends
with the /d/ sound.

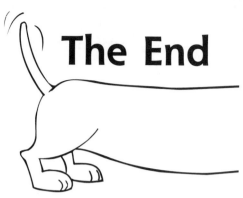

1. be d

2. li

3. mu

4. toa

5. mo

6. sle

7. po

8. tu

9. bir

**Adding the ending /d/ sound**

Name _____

If the picture name begins with the /d/ sound,
draw a line to the duck.

If the picture name ends with the /d/ sound,
draw a line to the pond.

# Duck Pond

**d**uck

pon**d**

Name _____

Write the letter **d** on the line that shows where you hear the /d/ sound.

# Beginning or End?

| | | |
|---|---|---|
| 1. <br> d__ og ____ | 2. <br> __ esk ____ | 3. <br> __ see ____ |
| 4. <br> __ eer ____ | 5. <br> __ sle ____ | 6. <br> __ bea ____ |
| 7. <br> __ ish ____ | 8. <br> __ toa ____ | 9. <br> __ ime ____ |

Completing words with the /d/ sound

**Beginning and Ending**
**Consonant Sounds**

Basic Phonics Skills, Level B • EMC 3319 • ©2004 by Evan-Moor Corp.

Name _____

Circle the picture if the name begins with the /h/ sound.

Hh

**h**appy

**h**en

**To the Teacher:** Review the picture names with students. (house, hat, hand, hoe, cat, hook)

**Recognizing the beginning /h/ sound**

**Beginning and Ending Consonant Sounds** **81**

Name _____

Glue the picture inside the heart if its name begins
with the /h/ sound.
Glue the picture outside the heart if its name does
not begin with the /h/ sound.

# Have a Heart

| glue | glue |
|------|------|
| glue | glue |

| glue | glue |
|------|------|

**Recognizing the beginning /h/ sound**

**Beginning and Ending Consonant Sounds**    Basic Phonics Skills, Level B • EMC 3319 • ©2004 by Evan-Moor Corp.

Name _____

Write the letter **h** if the word begins with the /h/ sound.
Draw lines to connect the pairs of words that go together.

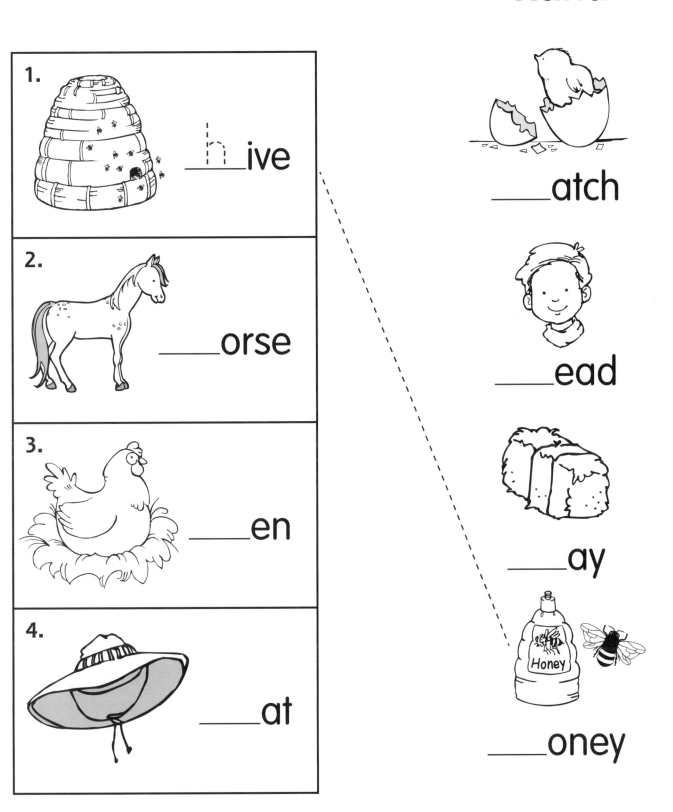

1. _h_ive

2. ___orse

3. ___en

4. ___at

___atch

___ead

___ay

___oney

Name _____

Hanna likes to help in the garden. Write the letter **h** on the lines where you hear the /h/ sound.

# Hanna Can Help

**1.**

h oe ____

**2.**

____at____

**3.**

____ook____

**4.**

____en____

**5.**

____orn____

**6.**

____ose____

**Completing words with the /h/ sound**

Name _____

Circle the picture if the name begins with the /g/ sound.

# Gray Goat

# Gg

**g**ray
**g**oat

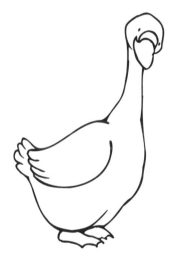

**To the Teacher:** Review the picture names with students.
(gate, girl, goose, gum, can, ghost)

**Recognizing the beginning /g/ sound**

Name _____

Write the letter **g** on the line if the picture begins with the /g/ sound.

# Go, Geese, Go!

1. __g__old

2. ___um

3. ___ate

4. ___oat

5. ___irl

6. ___at

**Adding the beginning /g/ sound**

**Beginning and Ending Consonant Sounds**

Basic Phonics Skills, Level B • EMC 3319 • ©2004 by Evan-Moor Corp.

Name _____

Cut out the pictures.
Glue the pictures next to the garden gate if their name begins with the /g/ sound.

# Garden Gate

**g**arden

| glue | glue |
|------|------|
| glue | glue |

Recognizing the beginning /g/ sound

Name _____

Write the letter **g** if the picture name ends
with the /g/ sound.

# Big Bag
# of Bugs

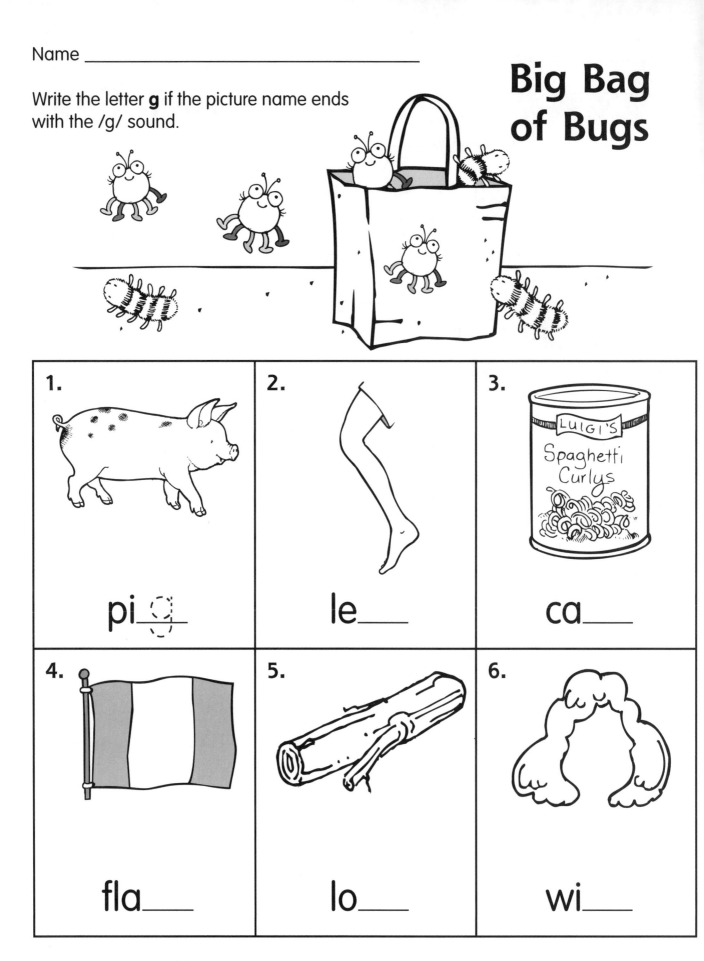

1. pi__g__

2. le____

3. ca____

4. fla____

5. lo____

6. wi____

Adding the ending /g/ sound

Beginning and Ending
**Consonant Sounds**

Name _____

If the picture name begins with the /g/ sound,
draw a line to the goose.

If the picture name ends with the /g/ sound,
draw a line to the egg.

# A Big Goose Egg

**g**oose

e**gg**

Name _____

What is your favorite pet?
Write the letter **g** on the lines where you hear
the /g/ sound.

# Guessing Game!

| | | |
|---|---|---|
| 1. | 2. | 3. |
| g_oose___ | ___do___ | ___fro___ |
| 4. | 5. | 6. |
| ___pi___ | ___oat___ | ___bu___ |

**Completing words with the /g/ sound**

Name _____

Say the name of each picture.
Listen for the beginning sound.
Draw a circle around the letter that stands for
the beginning sound.

| 1. | 2. | 3. |
|---|---|---|
| (d)  h  g | d  h  g | d  h  g |

| 4. | 5. | 6. |
|---|---|---|
| d  h  g | d  h  g | d  h  g |

| 7. | 8. | 9. |
|---|---|---|
| d  h  g | d  h  g | d  h  g |

Reviewing beginning sounds /d/ /h/ /g/

Name _____

Say the name of each picture.
Listen for the beginning sound.
Write the letter that stands for the beginning sound.

# More Review Beginning Sounds

## d h g

1.

2.

3.

4.

5.

6.

7.

8.

9.

**Reviewing beginning sounds /d/ /h/ /g/**

**Beginning and Ending Consonant Sounds**

Basic Phonics Skills, Level B • EMC 3319 • ©2004 by Evan-Moor Corp.

Name _____

Circle the picture in each row that has the same ending sound as the first picture.

©2004 by Evan-Moor Corp. • Basic Phonics Skills, Level B • EMC 3319

**Beginning and Ending Consonant Sounds** **93**

Name _____

Circle the picture if the word begins with the /l/ sound.

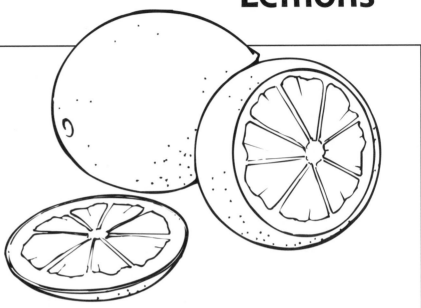

**Ll**
**lemons**

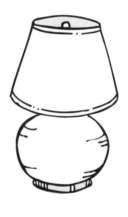

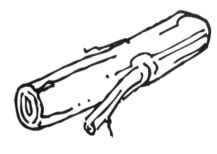

**To the Teacher:** Review the picture names with students.
(hand, lamp, leg, lip, lunchbox, log)

**Recognizing the beginning /l/ sound**

Name _____

Write the letter **l** if the picture name begins with the /l/ sound.

# Licking Lollipops

| 1. | 2. | 3. |
|---|---|---|
| __amp | __eaf | __ock |

| 4. | 5. | 6. |
|---|---|---|
| __ope | __ion | __adder |

Adding the beginning /l/ sound

Name _____

# A Snail Trail

Cut out the pictures. Glue the objects that end with the /l/ sound on the snail's shell. Glue the others under the snail.

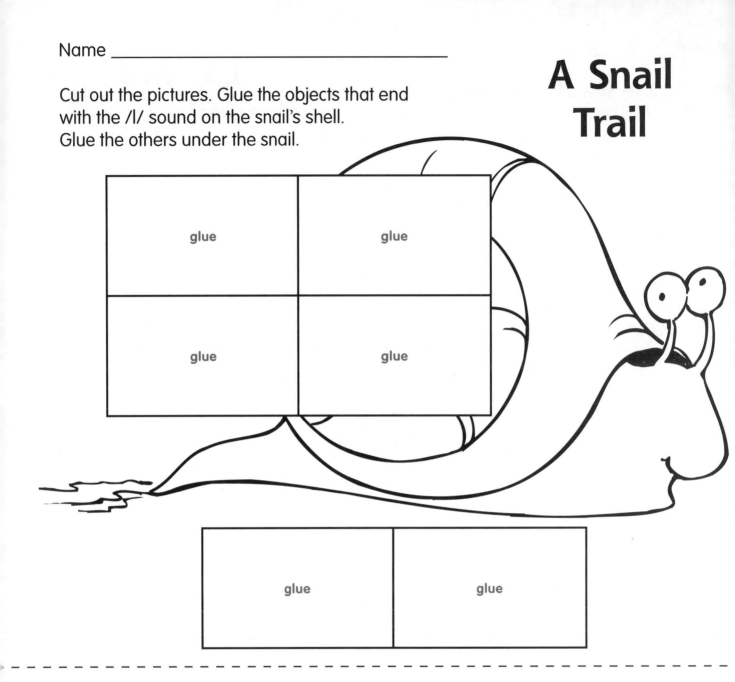

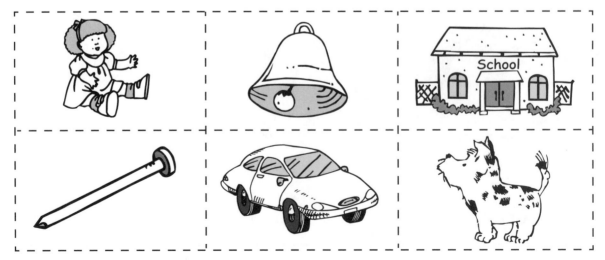

**Recognizing the ending /l/ sound**

**Beginning and Ending Consonant Sounds**

Basic Phonics Skills, Level B • EMC 3319 • ©2004 by Evan-Moor Corp.

Name _____

Write the letter **l** if the picture name ends
with the /l/ sound.

| | | |
|---|---|---|
| 1. poo_l_ | 2. bow___ | 3. whee___ |
| 4. wor___ | 5. hee___ | 6. sea___ |

**Adding the ending /l/ sound (spelled l)**

Name _____

Cut out the pictures.
Glue the picture by the lake if it begins with the /l/ sound.
Glue the picture by the pool if it ends with the /l/ sound.

# Lake or Pool?

lake

| glue | glue |
|------|------|
| glue | glue |

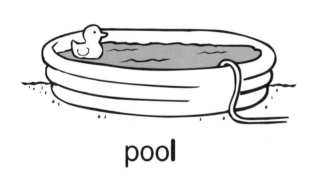

pool

| glue | glue |
|------|------|
| glue | glue |

**Distinguishing between the beginning and ending /l/ sound**

Basic Phonics Skills, Level B • EMC 3319 • ©2004 by Evan-Moor Corp.

Name _____

Write the letter **l** on the lines where
you hear the /l/ sound.

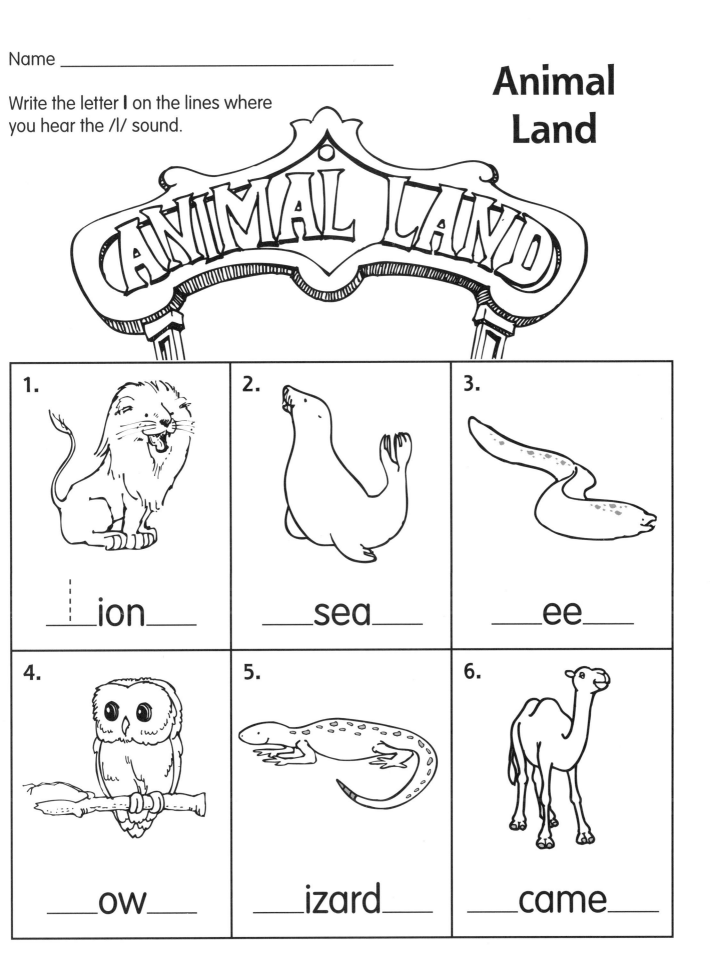

**1.** ___l___ion___

**2.** ___sea___

**3.** ___ee___

**4.** ___ow___

**5.** ___izard___

**6.** ___came___

**Completing words with the /l/ sound**

Name _____

Circle the picture in each row that has the
same ending sound as the first picture.

**Reviewing ending sounds /g/ /l/**

Beginning and Ending
**Consonant Sounds**

Basic Phonics Skills, Level B • EMC 3319 • ©2004 by Evan-Moor Corp.

Name _____

Circle the picture if the name begins
with the /j/ sound.

# Jj
## jump rope

**To the Teacher:** Review the picture names with students.
(jeep, jacks, jet, jelly beans, sun, jar)

**Recognizing the beginning /j/ sound**

Name _____

Look at each piece of the jigsaw puzzle.
Write the letter **j** if the picture name
begins with the /j/ sound.

# Jigsaw

j_am

___ug

___ar

___rum

___eep

___et

Adding the beginning /j/ sound (spelled j)

**Beginning and Ending
Consonant Sounds**                     Basic Phonics Skills, Level B • EMC 3319 • ©2004 by Evan-Moor Corp.

Name _____

Glue the pictures in the clouds if their name begins with the /j/ sound.

# Jumbo Jet

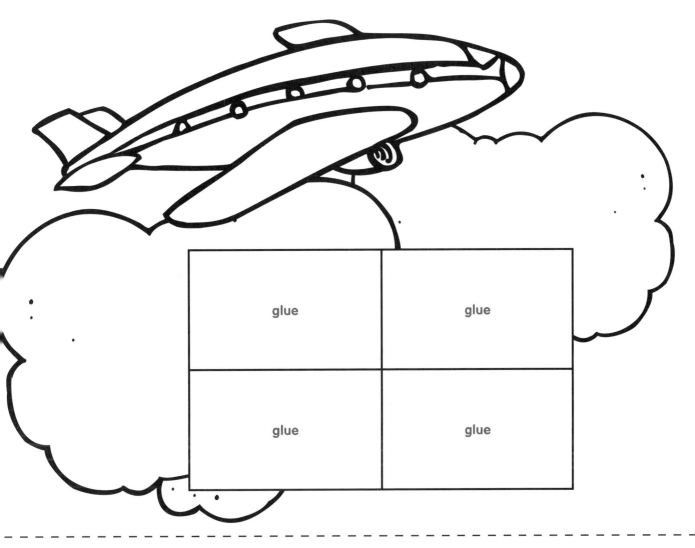

| glue | glue |
|------|------|
| glue | glue |

**Adding the beginning /j/ sound (spelled j)**

Beginning and Ending
**Consonant Sounds**

Name _____

Sometimes the letter **g** stands for the /j/ sound.
This is called the **soft g**.
Draw a line to the box that matches the beginning
sound of the picture.

# g or j?

**j** as in
jump rope

**g** as in
George
Washington

**g** as
in goat

**Recognizing the beginning /j/ sound (spelled j or g)**

Beginning and Ending
**Consonant Sounds**

Basic Phonics Skills, Level B • EMC 3319 • ©2004 by Evan-Moor Corp.

Name _____

Glue the words next to the correct picture.

# Gg

**g**ingerbread man

| | glue |
| --- | --- |
| | glue |
| | glue |

# Jj

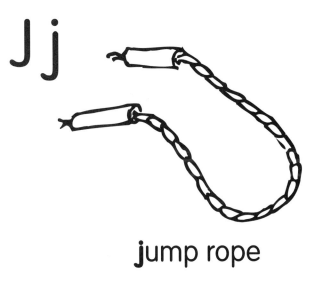

**j**ump rope

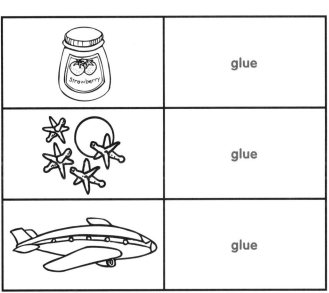

| | glue |
| --- | --- |
| | glue |
| | glue |

| giraffe | giant | jam |
| --- | --- | --- |
| gems | jet | jacks |

**Distinguishing between the beginning and ending /j/ sound (spelled j or g)**

Name _____

Circle the picture in each row that has the same ending sound as the first picture.

# Listen to the End

What do you hear at the beginning?

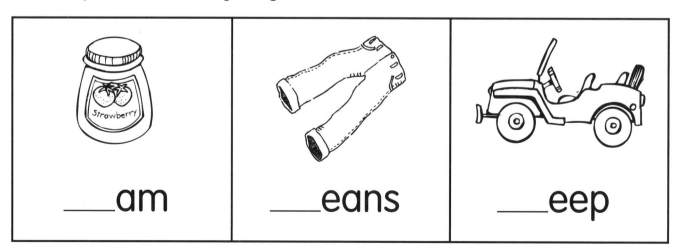

___am          ___eans          ___eep

**Completing words with the /j/ sound**

**Beginning and Ending**
**Consonant Sounds**

Name _____

Circle the picture if you hear the /n/ sound at the beginning.

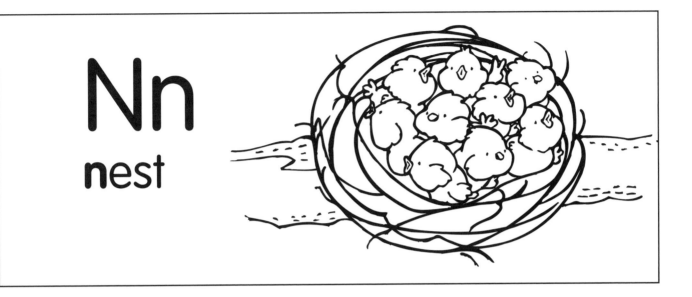

**Nn**
nest

**To the Teacher:** Review the picture names with students.
(nail, newspaper, nine, moon, nut, mouse)

**Recognizing the beginning /n/ sound**

**Beginning and Ending Consonant Sounds** 107

Name _____

Write the letter **n** if the picture name begins with the /n/ sound.

No!

| 1. | 2. | 3. |
|---|---|---|
| n̲eck | __amp | __ut |
| 4. | 5. | 6. |
| __et | __ote | __an |

**Adding the beginning /n/ sound**

Name _____

# A Queen's Crown

Cut out the pictures. Glue the pictures on the crown if their name ends with the /n/ sound.

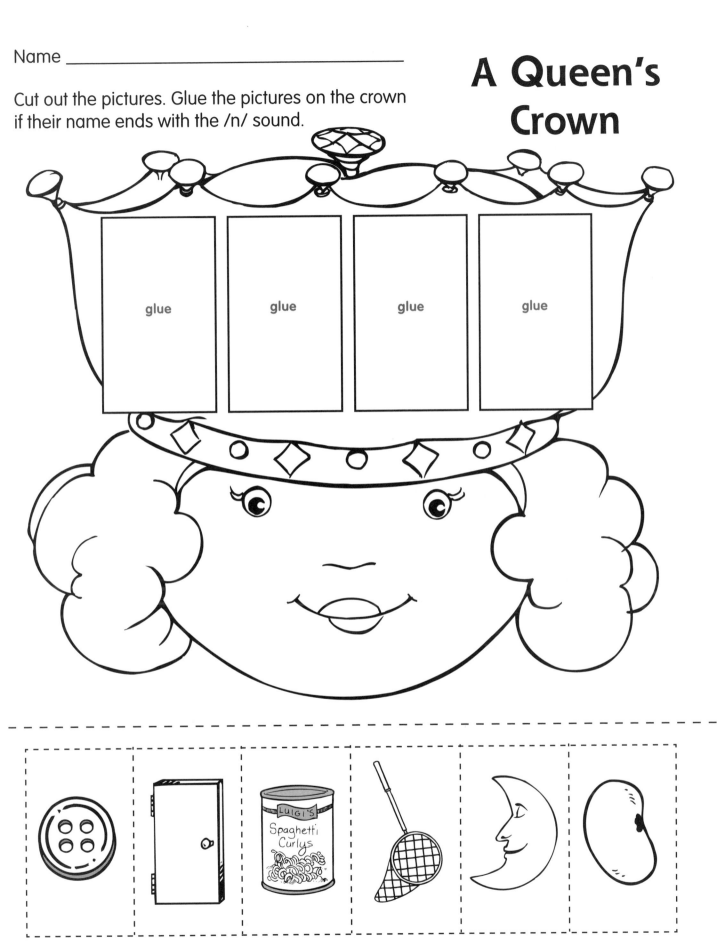

Name _____

Write the letter **n** if the picture name ends with the /n/ sound.

# Run, Run!

| | | |
|---|---|---|
| **1.**  trai_n_ | **2.**  boa___ | **3.**  wago___ |
| **4.**  va___ | **5.**  bu___ | **6.**  lio___ |

**Adding the ending /n/ sound**

**Beginning and Ending**
**Consonant Sounds**

Basic Phonics Skills, Level B • EMC 3319 • ©2004 by Evan-Moor Corp.

Name _____

Say the name of each picture.
Listen for the /n/ sound. Do you hear it
at the beginning or the end?
Write the letter **n** in the correct box.

# Nick Is Nice
# to Tin Tin

| 1. | 2. | 3. |
|---|---|---|
| | n | |

| 4. | 5. | 6. |
|---|---|---|
| | | |

**Distinguishing between the beginning and ending /n/ sound**

Beginning and Ending
**Consonant Sounds** 111

Name _____

Nan has a new kitten.
Write the letter **n** on the lines
where you hear the /n/ sound.

# Nan's New Kitten

| | | |
|---|---|---|
| 1.  | 2.  | 3.  |
| __pe__ n __ | __ickel__ | __est__ |
| 4.  | 5.  | 6.  |
| __ca__ | __trai__ | __ut__ |

**Completing words with the /n/ sound**

Name _____

Say the name of each picture.
Listen for the beginning sound.
Draw a circle around the letter that stands for the beginning sound.

| | | |
|---|---|---|
| **1.** | **2.** | **3.** |
| l j n | l j n | l j n |
| **4.** | **5.** | **6.** |
| l j n | l j n | l j n |
| **7.** | **8.** | **9.** |
| l j n | l j n | l j n |

Reviewing beginning sounds /l/ /j/ /n/

Name _____

Say the name of the first picture.
Listen for the beginning sound.
Write the letter that stands for that sound in the box.
Circle the object with the same beginning
sound in the row.

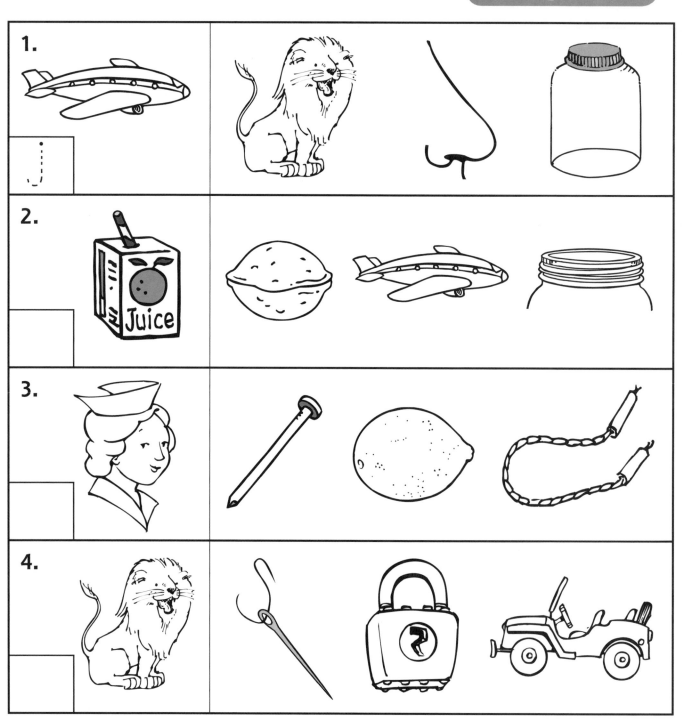

Reviewing beginning sounds /l/ /j/ /n/

**Beginning and Ending**
**Consonant Sounds**

Basic Phonics Skills, Level B • EMC 3319 • ©2004 by Evan-Moor Corp.

Name _____

Say the name of each picture.
Listen for the ending sound.
Draw a circle around the letter that stands
for the ending sound.

1.

l n

2.

l n

3.

l n

4.

l n

5.

l n

6.

l n

7.

l n

8.

l n

9.

LUIGI'S
Spaghetti
Curlys

l n

Reviewing ending sounds /l/ /n/

Name _____

Say the name of each picture.
Listen for the ending sound.
Write the letter that stands for the ending sound.

# More Review
# Ending
# Sounds

### l  n

1.

2.

3.

4.

5.

6.

7.

8.

9.

Name _____

Circle the picture if you hear the /w/ sound at the beginning.

**Ww**
**w**indow

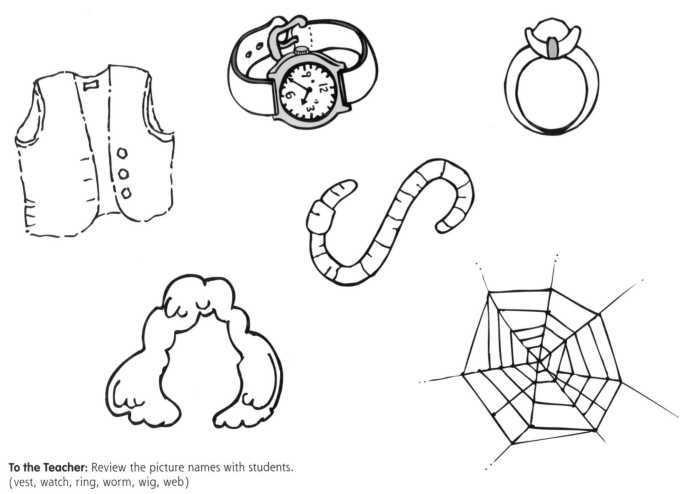

**To the Teacher:** Review the picture names with students.
(vest, watch, ring, worm, wig, web)

**Recognizing the beginning /w/ sound**

Name _____

Write the letter **w** if the picture name begins
with the /w/ sound.

# Walking on the Wall

| | | |
|---|---|---|
| 1. __w_asp | 2. ___ig | 3. ___ell |
| 4. ___olf | 5. ___ug | 6. ___ood |

**Adding the beginning /w/ sound**

Name _____

# Wendy's Wand

Wendy has a wishing wand.
She can change an object just by wishing.
Say the name of each object on the left.
Change the beginning sound to /w/.
Write the new word on the lines.

| | | |
|---|---|---|
| **1.** pig | | w  i  g |
| **2.** cave | | ___ ___ ___ ___ |
| **3.** ball | | ___ ___ ___ ___ |
| **4.** sing | | ___ ___ ___ ___ |
| **5.** net | | ___ ___ ___ |

**Completing words with the /w/ sound**

Name _____

Circle the picture if you hear the /y/ sound at the beginning.

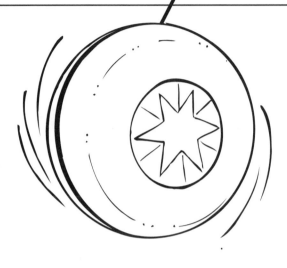

**Yy**
**y**ellow
**y**o-**y**o

**To the Teacher:** Review the picture names with students.
(yak, sun, yolk, yarn, kite, yawn)

**Recognizing the beginning /y/ sound**

Name _____

Write the letter **y** if the picture name
begins with the /y/ sound.

# A Yard of Yarn

| | | |
|---|---|---|
| 1. __y__arn | 2. ___ar | 3. ___awn |
| 4. ___o-___o | 5. ___ak | 6. ___ig |

**Adding the beginning /y/ sound**

Name _____

# Yolanda Can Yell!

Look at the pictures and write the beginning sound. Change the beginning sound of each word to /y/.

Write the letter **y** on the lines to make the new words.

| Write the beginning sound. | Change the beginning sound. | Draw a picture. |
|---|---|---|
| **1.** <br> _b_arn | _y_arn | |
| **2.** <br> ___awn | ___awn | |
| **3.** <br> ___am | ___am | |
| **4.** <br> ___ard | ___ard | |

**Completing words with the /y/ sound**

Basic Phonics Skills, Level B • EMC 3319 • ©2004 by Evan-Moor Corp.

Name _____

Circle the pictures that begin like **quilt**.

# Qq
quilt

**To the Teacher:** Review the picture names with students.
(can, quarter, question mark, queen, quail, cake)

**Recognizing the beginning /kw/ sound**

Name _____

Change the beginning sound of each word to /kw/.
Write the letters **qu** on the lines to make the
new words.

# Quick Quiz

| | Say the word. | Change the beginning sound. | Draw a picture. |
|---|---|---|---|
| **1.** | pail | q̲ u̲ail | |
| **2.** | tack | __ __ack | |
| **3.** | teen | __ __een | |
| **4.** | tick | __ __ick | |

The letters **qu** usually stand for the **/kw/** sound when they are at the beginning of a word.

Name _____

Listen to your teacher read each question.
Write the letters **qu** on the lines where you hear
the /kw/ sound.

# Questions

| | | |
|---|---|---|
| **1.** | What does a duck say? | q u ack |
| **2.** | What should you be if a baby is sleeping? | __ __ iet |
| **3.** | What do you call one of the sharp things on a porcupine? | __ __ ill |
| **4.** | What is another name for a test? | __ __ iz |

Completing words with the /kw/ sound

Beginning and Ending
**Consonant Sounds** 125

Name _____

Circle the pictures that begin like **zebra**.

# Zz
**z**ebra

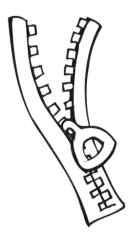

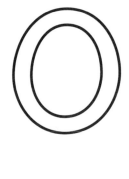

**To the Teacher:** Review the picture names with students.
(sun, zipper, zero, sled, zoo)

**Recognizing the beginning /z/ sound**

Name _____

Write the letter **z** if the picture name begins with the /z/ sound.

# ZZZ

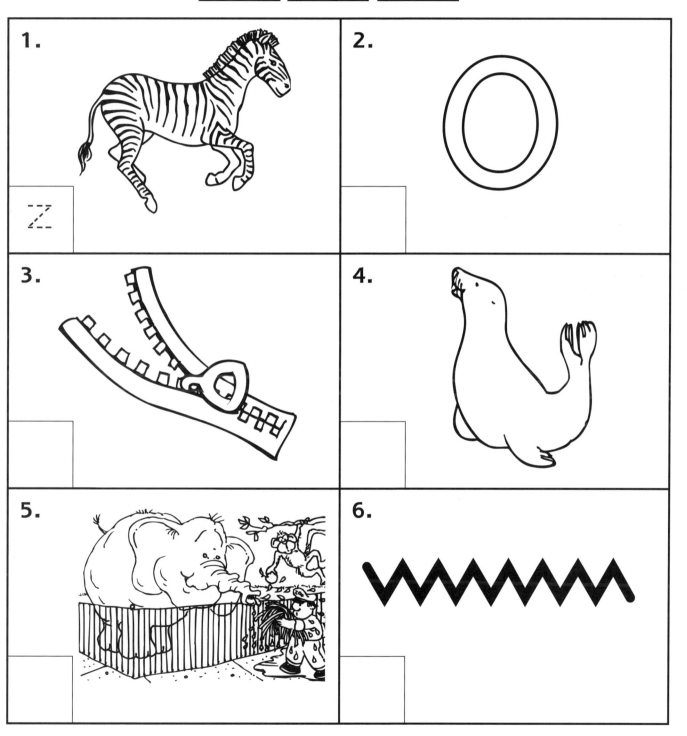

1. z

2.

3.

4.

5.

6.

Adding the beginning /z/ sound

Name _____

Write the letter **z** if the picture name begins with the /z/ sound.

**z**oo

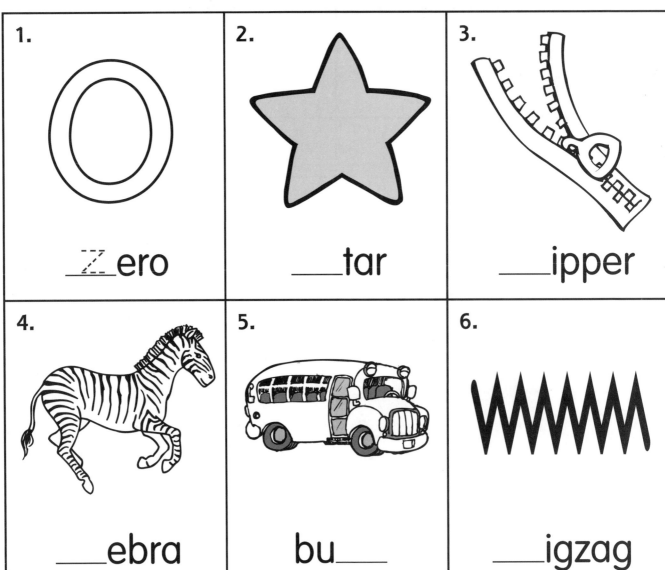

1. __z__ero

2. ___tar

3. ___ipper

4. ___ebra

5. bu___

6. ___igzag

Recognizing the beginning /z/ sound

Name _____

Write the letters **z** or **zz** where you hear the /z/ sound.

# Fuzz? Buzz?

| | |
|---|---|
| **1.**<br><br>A peach has<br>fu __z__ __z__. | **2.**<br><br>A light wind is<br>a bree____e. |
| **3.**<br><br>A bee says<br>bu ____ ____. | **4.**<br><br>A blue ribbon is<br>for first pri____e. |
| **5.**<br><br>The teacher gave<br>us a qui____. | **6.**<br><br>A glass of soda<br>has fi____ ____. |

Adding the ending /z/ sound (spelled z or zz)

Name _____

Fill in the circle on the left if you hear the /z/ sound at the beginning.

Fill in the circle on the right if you hear the /z/ sound at the end.

# Listen for z

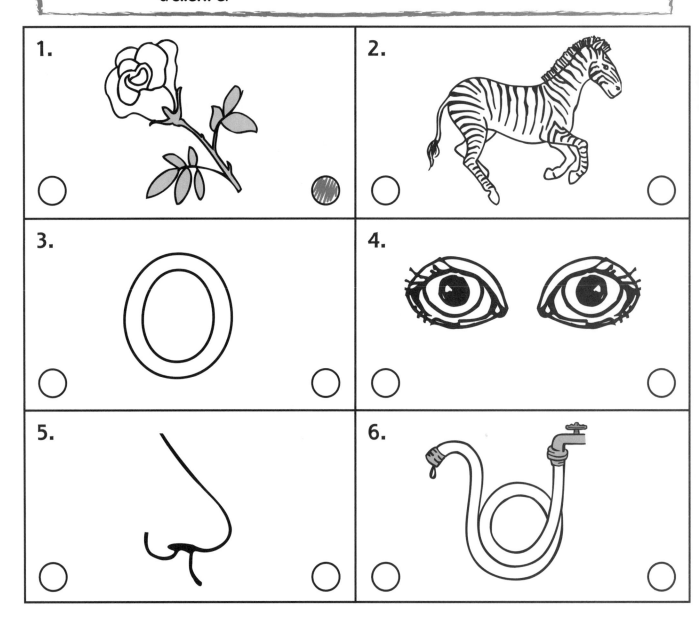

1.

○          ●

2.

○          ○

3.

○          ○

4.

○          ○

5.

○          ○

6.

○          ○

**Distinguishing between the beginning and ending /z/ sound**

Name _____

Write the correct letter(s) **z, zz,** or **s** on the lines where you hear the /z/ sound.

# Zigzag

| | | |
|---|---|---|
| **1.** 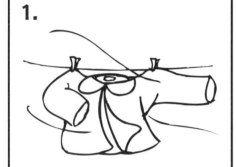 | **2.**  | **3.**  |
| bree__z__e | bu__ __ __ | ro___e |
| **4.**  | **5.**  | **6.**  |
| tree___ | ___oom | ___oo |

**Completing words with the /z/ sound**

Name _____

Circle **yes** if you hear the /x/ sound at the beginning.

# Extra! Extra! Read All About It!

**1.** window

yes      (no)

**2.** tree

yes      no

**3.** X ray

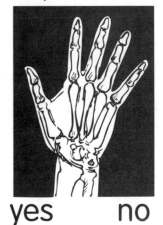

yes      no

**4.** exercise

yes      no

**5.** shoe

yes      no

**6.** exit

yes      no

**Recognizing the beginning sounds /eks/ and /z/ (spelled x)**

Name _____

# Fix the Mix

Cut out and glue the pictures to the mixing bowl if they end with the /x/ sound.

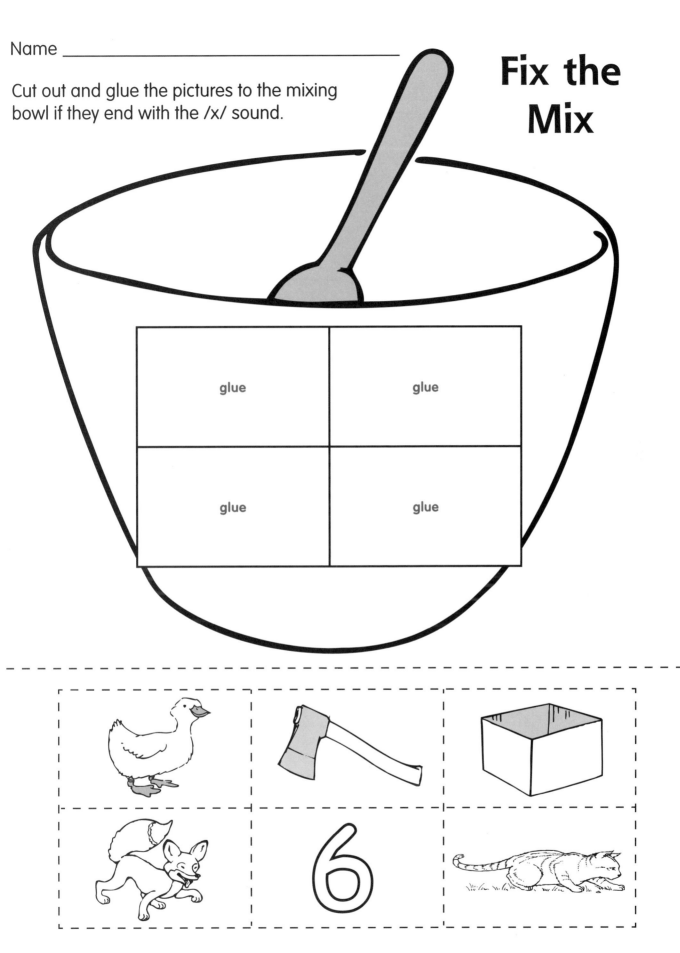

| | |
|---|---|
| glue | glue |
| glue | glue |

**Beginning and Ending**
**Consonant Sounds** 133

Name _____

Write the letter **x** on the lines where
you hear the /eks/ or /ks/ sound.

# Max Is Six

| | | |
|---|---|---|
| **1.** | **2.** | **3.** |
| bo_x_ | si___ | ___ ray |
| **4.** | **5.** | **6.** |
| ___un | fo___ | ___at |

**Phonics Fact!** The letter **x** at the end of a word usually stands for the /ks/ sound.

**Adding the beginning /eks/ sound and the ending /ks/ sound**

Basic Phonics Skills, Level B • EMC 3319 • ©2004 by Evan-Moor Corp.

Name _____

Look at the first picture. Read the word.
Change the ending sound to /ks/.
Write the new word using the letter **x**.

# X-Change

| | | |
|---|---|---|
| **1.** | tag | ta_x_ |
| **2.** | fin | fi___ |
| **3.** | saw | sa___ |
| **4.** | sit | si___ |
| **5.** | tub | tu___ |
| **6.** | bow | bo___ |

**Completing words with the /eks/ or /ks/ sound**

Name _____

Say the name of each picture.
Circle the letter or letters that stand
for the beginning sound.

# Review Beginning Sounds

## qu w x y z

1.
(qu) w x y z

2.
qu w x y z

3.
qu w x y z

4.
qu w x y z

5.
qu w x y z

6.
qu w x y z

7.
qu w x y z

8.
qu w x y z

9.
qu w x y z

Review beginning sounds /qu/ /w/ /x/ /y/ /z/

Basic Phonics Skills, Level B • EMC 3319 • ©2004 by Evan-Moor Corp.

Name _____

Say the name of each picture.
Listen for the beginning sound.
Write it in the box.

| | | |
|---|---|---|
| **1.** <br> W | **2.** | **3.** |
| **4.** | **5.** | **6.** |
| **7.** | **8.** | **9.** |

Review beginning sounds /qu/ /w/ /x/ /y/ /z/

Name _____

Say the name of each picture.
Listen for the ending sound.
Draw a circle around the letter that stands for the ending sound.

| 1. | 2. | 3. |
|---|---|---|
| z  (x) | z  x | z  x |
| 4. | 5. | 6. |
| z  x | z  x | z  x |
| 7. | 8. | 9. |
| z  x | z  x | z  x |

**Review ending sounds /z/ /x/**

# Short Vowel Sounds

Name _____

Each sound in English is represented by a letter or set of letters. Each letter is either a vowel or a consonant. The letters **a, e, i, o,** and **u** are vowels. The other 21 letters are called consonants.

Color each of the vowels red.
Color each of the consonants blue.

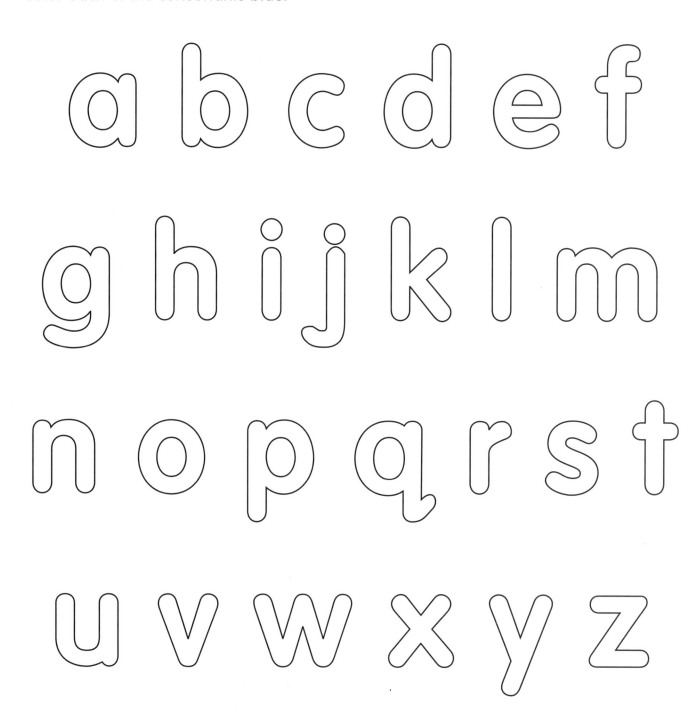

**Distinguishing consonants from vowels**

Name _____

Circle the picture if you hear the **short a** sound.

# Dad's Van

**Aa**

van

Dad has a tan van.

**To the Teacher:** Review the picture names with students.
(cap, pig, map, rat, rose, bat)

**Recognizing the short a sound /ă/**

Name _____

Say the sound each letter stands for.
Follow the arrow to blend the sounds.
Draw a line from the word to the picture it names.

# Say It

1. **m a p**

2. **b a t**
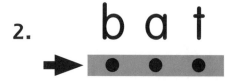

3. **f a n**

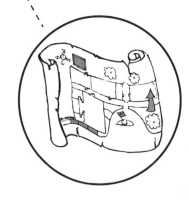

4. **b a g**
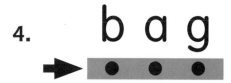

5. **h a t**

**Blending and matching words with the short a sound /ă/**

Basic Phonics Skills, Level B • EMC 3319 • ©2004 by Evan-Moor Corp.

Name _____

# Unscramble It

Say the name of the picture.
Unscramble the letters. Write the word.

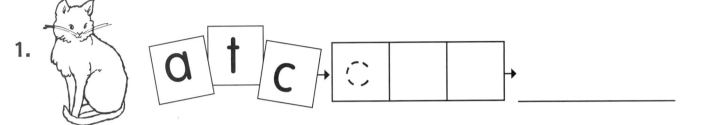

1. a t c → ◌ ☐ ☐ → _____

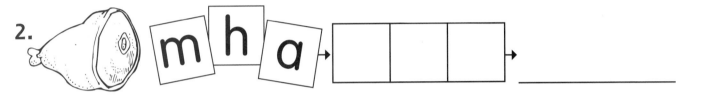

2. m h a → ☐ ☐ ☐ → _____

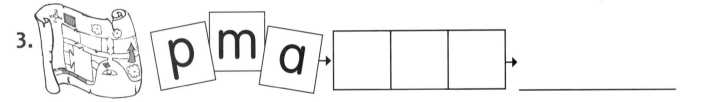

3. p m a → ☐ ☐ ☐ → _____

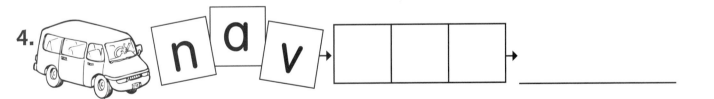

4. n a v → ☐ ☐ ☐ → _____

5. a j m → ☐ ☐ ☐ → _____

**Blending and writing words with the short a sound /ă/**

Name _____

Say the name of the picture.
Find the letters. Write the word.

# Find the Letters

| a | b | c | f | g | h | n | t |

1.

2.

3.

4.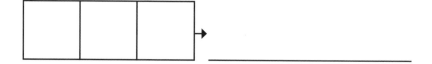

5.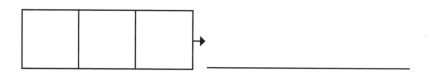

**Blending and writing words with the short a sound /ă/**

Basic Phonics Skills, Level B • EMC 3319 • ©2004 by Evan-Moor Corp.

Name _____

Find the correct word in the word box.
Write the word on the lines.

# Match It Up

| ram | rat | man |
|-----|-----|-----|
| pan | tag | cap |

**1.**

c a p

**2.**

_ _ _

**3.**

_ _ _

**4.**

_ _ _

**5.**

_ _ _

**6.**

_ _ _

**Writing words with the short a sound /ă/**

Name _____

Listen to the beginning, middle, and ending sounds. Write the word on the lines.

# Write It

1. c a n

2. ___ ___ ___

3. ___ ___ ___

4. ___ ___ ___

5. ___ ___ ___

6. ___ ___ ___

**Writing words with the short a sound /ă/**

Basic Phonics Skills, Level B • EMC 3319 • ©2004 by Evan-Moor Corp.

Name _____

Circle the word that best completes the sentence.
Write the word on the line.

# Questions?

1.

Dad had a _____n a p_____ .

wag    pat    (nap)

2.

The _____ ran fast.

cat    tag    ham

3.

Nan is _____ .

map    fan    sad

4.

Jack has a _____ .

can    bag    mat

Writing short a words to complete sentences

Name _____

A sentence always starts with an uppercase letter. Most sentences end with a period (.). Put the words in the correct order. Write the sentence on the line.

# Ann, Jan, and Max

| | |
|---|---|
| **1.** | a ran can Ann by<br><br>Ann _____ |
| **2.** | Jan a ham has<br><br>_____ |
| **3.** | mad is Jan Max at<br><br>_____ |
| **4.** | the pat cat Ann can<br><br>_____ |

**Writing sentences with short a words**

Basic Phonics Skills, Level B • EMC 3319 • ©2004 by Evan-Moor Corp.

Name _____

Read each sentence. Draw a line to match the sentence to the correct picture.

1. Pat ran and ran.

2. I am mad.

3. An ant sat.

4. Dan can fan.

5. Cat had a bag.

6. Fat rat has a pan.

Reading short a words

Name _____

Cut out the pictures.
Glue the pictures that have a **short a** sound
in the boxes.

# Find Short a

fat cat

| glue | glue |
|------|------|
| glue | glue |

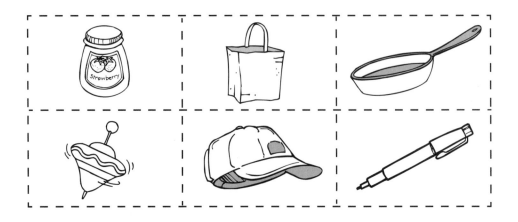

**Identifying short a words**

Name _____

Circle the word that names the picture.

I am a jam fan.

| | | |
|---|---|---|
| **1.**   | man <br> (can) <br> cab | |
| **2.**  | bad <br> bag <br> wag | |
| **3.**  | jan <br> ram <br> jam | |

**1.**   man / (can) / cab

**2.**   bad / bag / wag

**3.**   jan / ram / jam

**4.**   sat / dad / sad

**5.**   tan / pan / pad

**6.**   hat / mat / ham

**7.**   cat / cap / rat

**8.**   ran / van / vat

**9.**   mad / lap / map

Review and assessment of short a words

Name _____

Circle the picture if you hear the **short i** sound.

# Tim's Pig

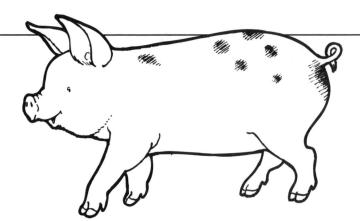

**Ii**
pig

Tim's pig **is** pink.

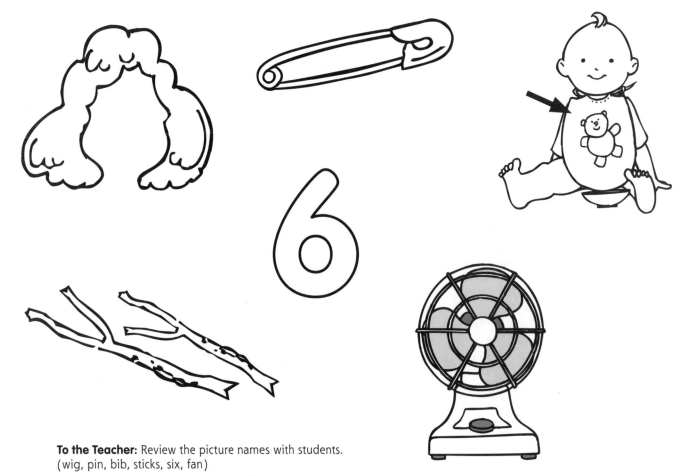

**To the Teacher:** Review the picture names with students.
(wig, pin, bib, sticks, six, fan)

**Recognizing the short i sound /ĭ/**

Basic Phonics Skills, Level B • EMC 3319 • ©2004 by Evan-Moor Corp.

Name _____

Say the sound each letter stands for.
Follow the arrow to blend the sounds.
Draw a line from the word to the picture it names.

# Say It

1.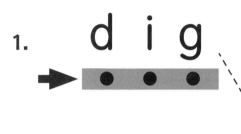

2.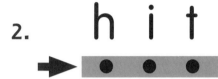

3.

4.

5.

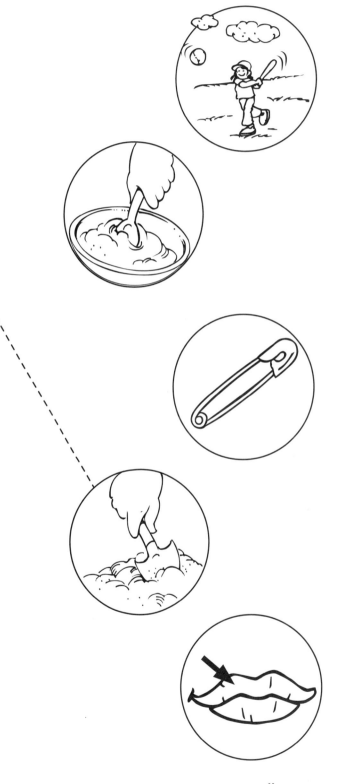

Blending and matching words with the short i sound /ĭ/

Name _____

Say the name of the picture.
Unscramble the letters.
Write the word.

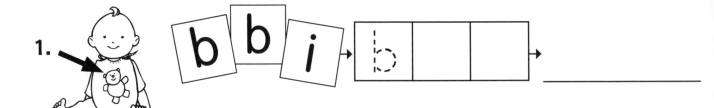

1. b b i → b ☐ ☐ → _____

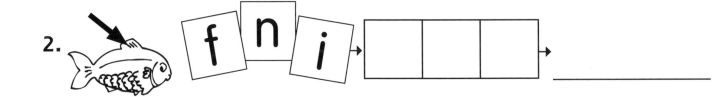

2. f n i → ☐ ☐ ☐ → _____

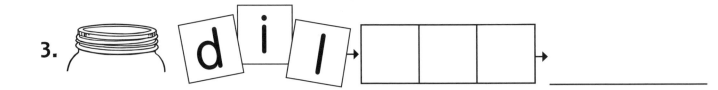

3. d i l → ☐ ☐ ☐ → _____

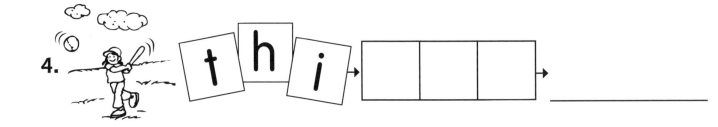

4. t h i → ☐ ☐ ☐ → _____

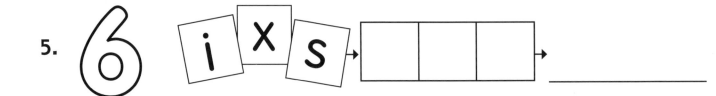

5. i x s → ☐ ☐ ☐ → _____

**Phonics Fact!** Words that follow the CVC pattern have a short vowel.

**Blending and writing words with the short i sound /ĭ/**

Name _____

Say the name of the picture.
Find the letters.
Write the word.

| i | b | g | p | r | w |
|---|---|---|---|---|---|

1.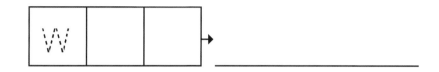

w | | → _____

2.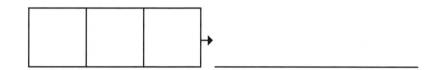

| | | → _____

3.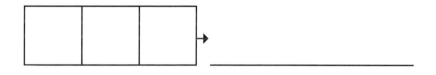

| | | → _____

4.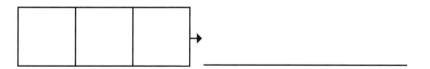

| | | → _____

5.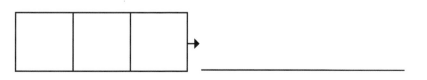

| | | → _____

**Blending and writing words with the short i sound /ĭ/**

Name _____

Find the correct word in the word box.
Write the word on the lines.

# Match It Up

| | | |
|---|---|---|
| six | zip | pin |
| wig | fin | lid |

**1.**

z i p

**2.**

6

____

**3.**

____

**4.**

____

**5.**

____

**6.**

____

**Writing words with the short i sound /ĭ/**

Name _____

Listen to the beginning, middle,
and ending sounds.
Write the word on the lines.

# Tib's Bib

Tib **is in** a bib.

---

**1.**

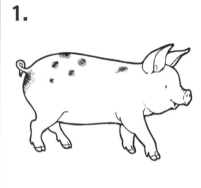

p i g

**2.**

___ ___ ___

**3.**

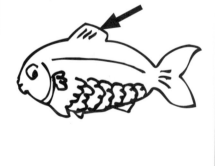

___ ___ ___

**4.**

___ ___ ___

**5.**

___ ___ ___

**6.**

___ ___ ___

---

**Writing words with the short i sound /ĭ/**

Name _____

Fill in the circle beside the word that best completes the sentence.
Write the word on the line.

# What Is It?

1.

It is a big _____.

○ fix  ● pig  ○ rib

2.

Liz can _____ it.

○ hit  ○ six  ○ wig

3.

It did not _____.

○ fit  ○ fin  ○ pit

4.

Liz likes to _____.

○ sip  ○ sit  ○ him

**Writing short i words to complete sentences**

Basic Phonics Skills, Level B • EMC 3319 • ©2004 by Evan-Moor Corp.

Name _____

Unscramble the words. Write the sentence on the line.

# Fix It!

1.

   can Tim hit

   Tim _____

2.

   bib Sis a has

   _____

3.

   win the can pig

   _____

4.

   dig can Vic pit a

   _____

**Writing sentences with short i words**

Name _____

Read each sentence. Draw a line to match the sentence to the correct picture.

# Reading Short i Words

1. Jim can dig.

2. Liz is big.

3. Kit is in the pit.

4. It will sit in the lid.

5. Lick the stick.

6. The wig fits Pig.

Reading short i words

Basic Phonics Skills, Level B • EMC 3319 • ©2004 by Evan-Moor Corp.

Name _____

Cut out the pictures. Listen for the vowel sounds.
Glue the pictures by the pig or the cat.

# Listen for the Vowels

big pig

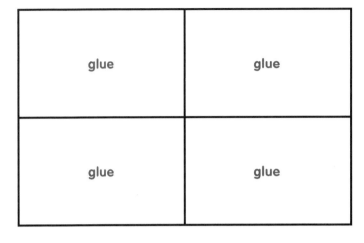

| glue | glue |
| glue | glue |

fat cat

| glue | glue |
| glue | glue |

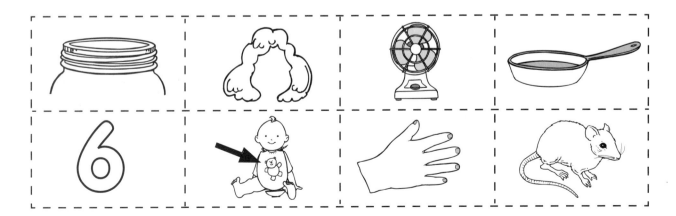

**Identifying short i and short a words**

Name _____

Circle the word that names the picture.

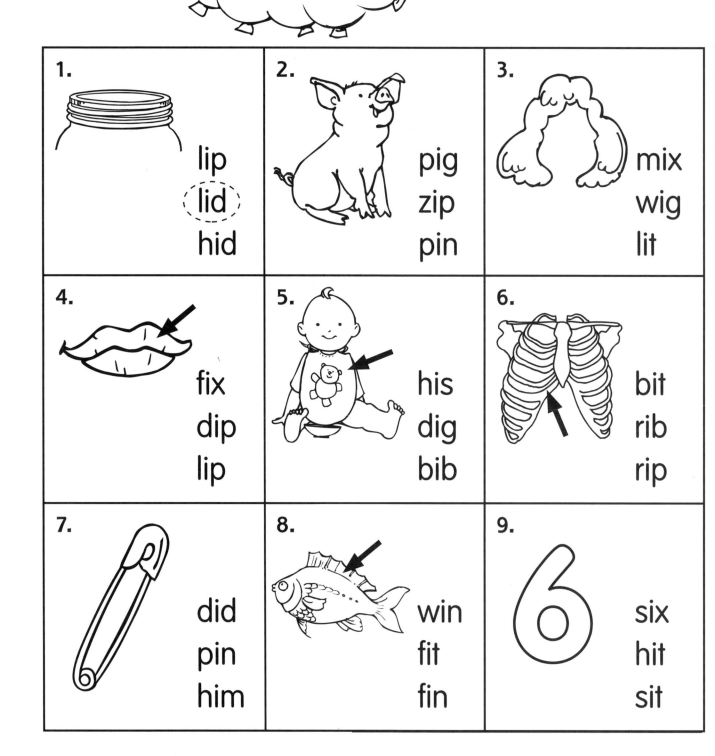

1.
lip
(lid)
hid

2.
pig
zip
pin

3.
mix
wig
lit

4.
fix
dip
lip

5.
his
dig
bib

6.
bit
rib
rip

7.
did
pin
him

8.
win
fit
fin

9.
six
hit
sit

**Review and assessment of short i words**

Basic Phonics Skills, Level B • EMC 3319 • ©2004 by Evan-Moor Corp.

Name _____

Listen for the **short a** or **short i** sound.
Write the correct letter on the line to
complete the word.

# Big or Bag?

| 1.  c_t | 2.  b__g | 3.  s__x |
|---|---|---|
| 4.  r__p | 5.  v__n | 6.  l__p |
| 7.  w__g | 8.  p__n | 9. 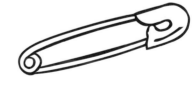 p__n |

**Distinguishing between short a and short i sounds**

Name _____

Circle the picture if you hear the **short o** sound.

# Oo
**fox**

**F**ox is **o**n a b**o**x.

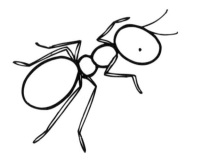

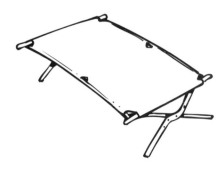

**To the Teacher:** Review the picture names with students.
(pot, ant, cot, dot, cup, mop)

**Recognizing the short o sound /ŏ/**

Name _____

Say the sound each letter stands for.
Follow the arrow to blend the sounds.
Draw a line from the word to the picture it names.

# Say It

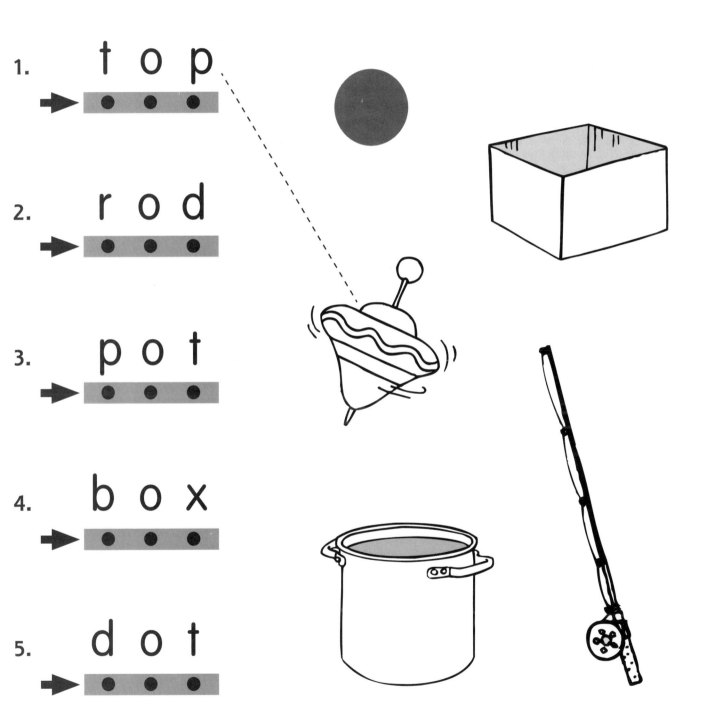

1. t o p

2. r o d

3. p o t

4. b o x

5. d o t

Name _____

Say the name of the picture.
Unscramble the letters.
Write the word.

1.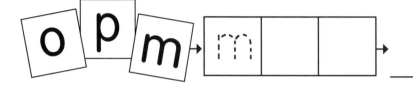

o p m → m ___ ___ → _____

2.

t h o → ___ ___ ___ → _____

3.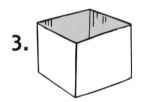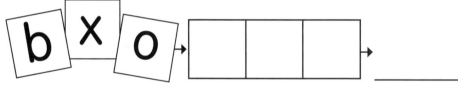

b x o → ___ ___ ___ → _____

4. o t c → ___ ___ ___ → _____

5. b c o → ___ ___ ___ → _____

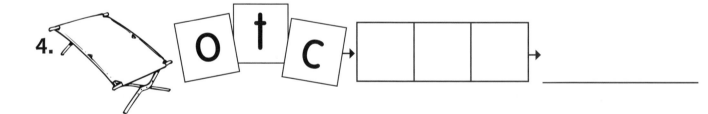

**Phonics Fact!** Words that follow the CVC pattern have a short vowel.

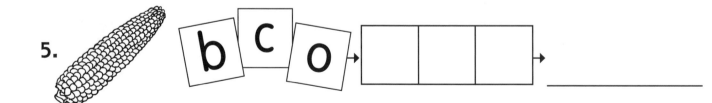

**Blending and writing words with the short o sound /ŏ/**

**166** Short Vowel Sounds

Basic Phonics Skills, Level B • EMC 3319 • ©2004 by Evan-Moor Corp.

Name _____

Say the name of the picture.
Find the letters.
Write the word.

# Find the Letters

| o | d | g | h | p | r | t |

**1.**

| d |  |  | → _____

**2.**

|  |  |  | → _____

**3.**

|  |  |  | → _____
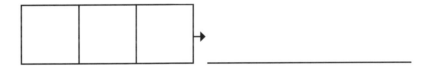

**4.**

|  |  |  | → _____
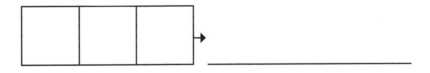

**5.**

|  |  |  | → _____
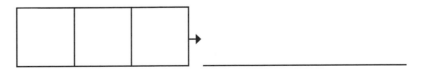

**Blending and writing words with the short o sound /ŏ/**

Name _____

Find the correct word in the word box.
Write the word on the lines.

# Match It Up

| log | fox | hot |
| pot | mop | cob |

**1.**

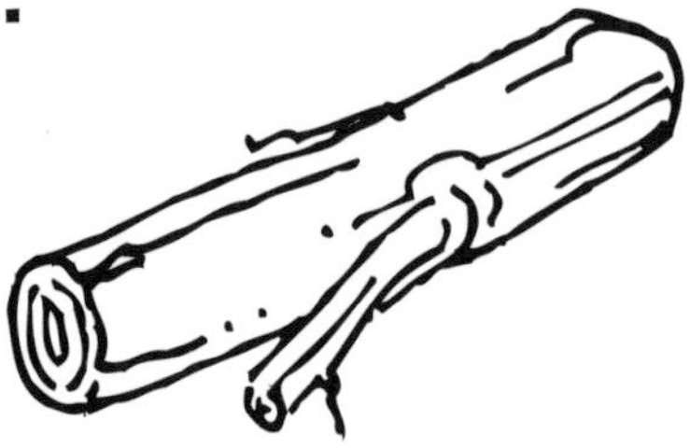

l o g

**2.**

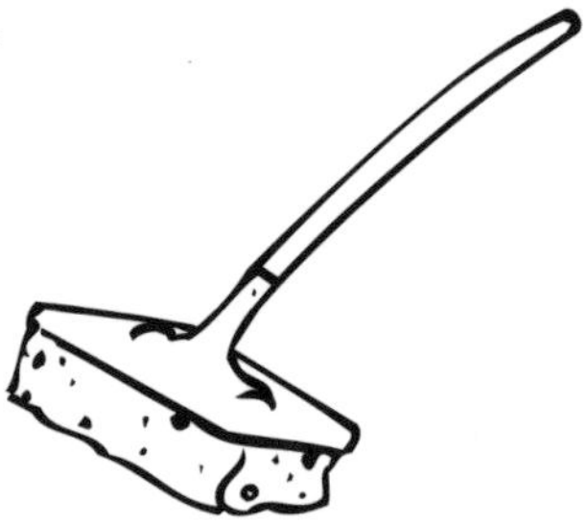

_ _ _

**3.**

_ _ _

**4.**

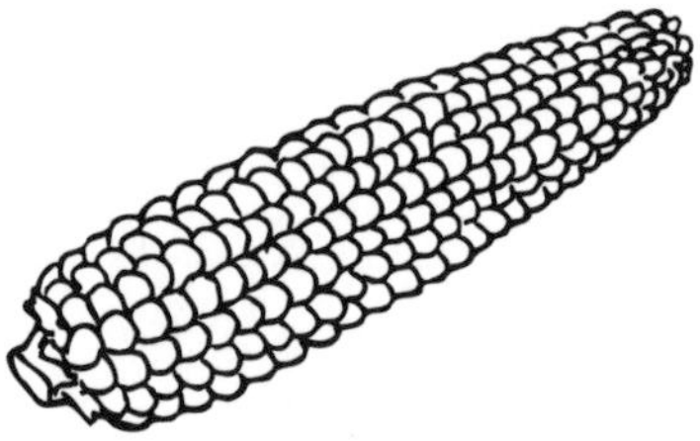

_ _ _

**5.**

_ _ _

**6.**

_ _ _

Writing words with the short o sound /ŏ/

Name _____

Listen to the beginning, middle, and ending sounds.
Write the word on the lines.

# Bob's Dog

Bob's dog is tops.

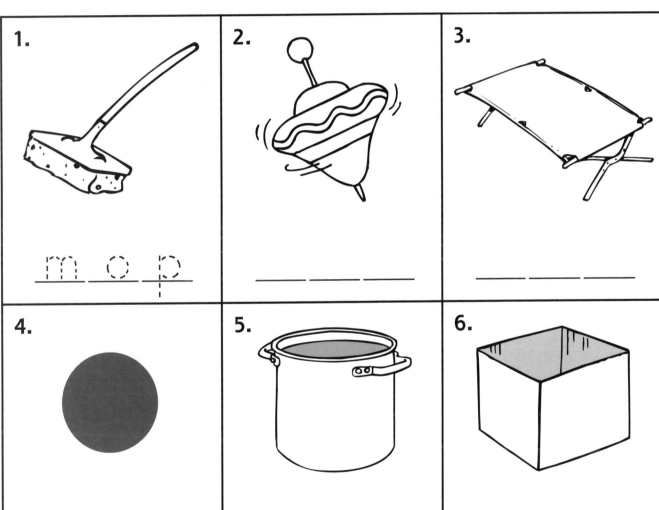

1.

m o p

2.

_ _ _

3.

_ _ _

4.

_ _ _

5.

_ _ _

6.

_ _ _

Name _____

Fill in the circle beside the word that best completes the sentence. Write the word on the line.

# The Short o

1. Tom got a _____.

   ○ pot      ○ rod      ○ box

2. The lid is on the _____.

   ○ pot      ○ mop      ○ hot

3. A _____ is on a log.

   ○ dot      ○ fog      ○ fox

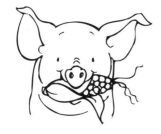

4. The hog has a _____.

   ○ cob      ○ dog      ○ cot

**Writing short o words to complete sentences**

Basic Phonics Skills, Level B • EMC 3319 • ©2004 by Evan-Moor Corp.

Name _____

Put the words in the correct order to make a sentence that asks a question. Write the question on the line.

# Can You Do It?

> **Remember –** A sentence that asks a question always ends with a question mark (**?**).

| | |
|---|---|
| **1.** | lock did Don it<br><br>Did _____ |
| **2.** | is Mom hot<br><br>_____ |
| **3.** | dot the is top on<br><br>_____ |
| **4.** | the in the fog is dog<br><br>_____ |

**Writing sentences with short o words**

Name _____

Read each sentence. Draw a line to match the sentence to the correct picture.

# Reading Short o Words

1. Dot got a dog.

2. Frog hopped on a rock.

3. Do not drop the box.

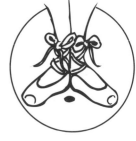

4. Stop on the dot.

5. Fox got a lock.

6. Hog is not hot.

Basic Phonics Skills, Level B • EMC 3319 • ©2004 by Evan-Moor Corp.

Name _____

Cut out the pictures.
Listen for the vowel sounds.
Glue the pictures by the fox or the pig.

**fox on a box**

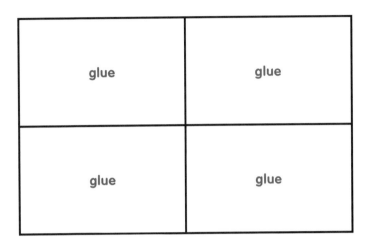

| glue | glue |
|------|------|
| glue | glue |

**big pig**

| glue | glue |
|------|------|
| glue | glue |

**Identifying short o and short i words**

Name ______________________________

# Short Vowel Review

## short o

Circle the word that names the picture.

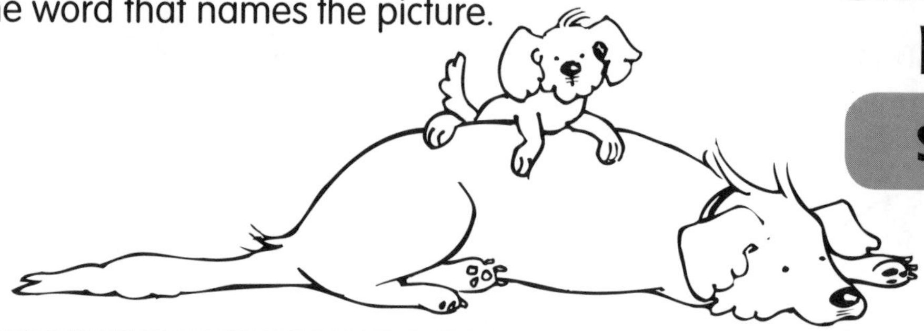

| | | |
|---|---|---|
| 1.  pop<br>pod<br>rod | 2.  hog<br>sob<br>log | 3.  mom<br>hop<br>mop |
| 4.  lot<br>cot<br>cob | 5.  top<br>pot<br>not | 6.  box<br>hog<br>hot |
| 7.  dot<br>dog<br>hot | 8.  dog<br>box<br>fox | 9.  cot<br>pot<br>box |

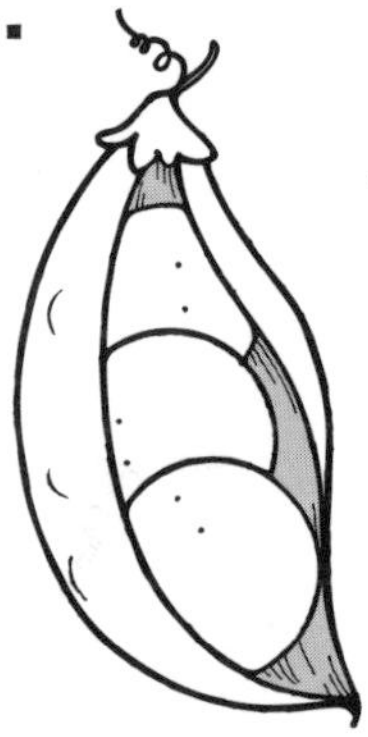

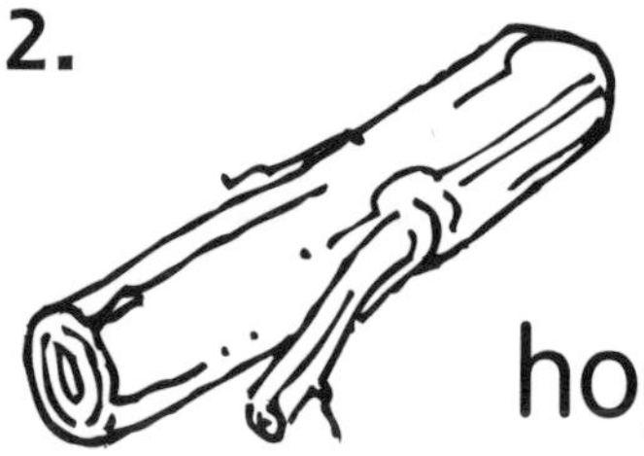

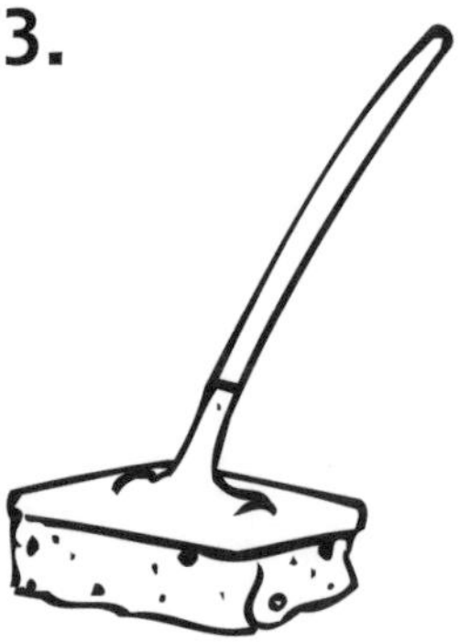

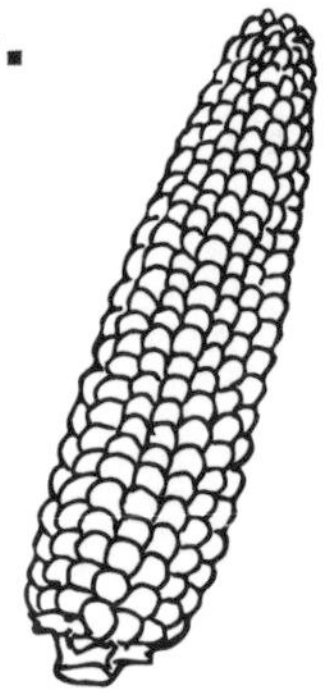

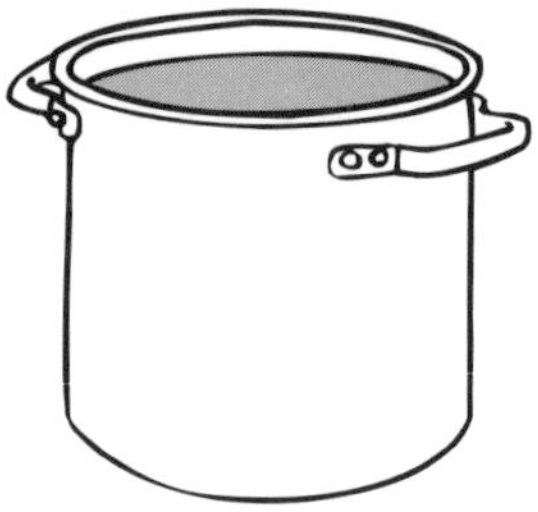

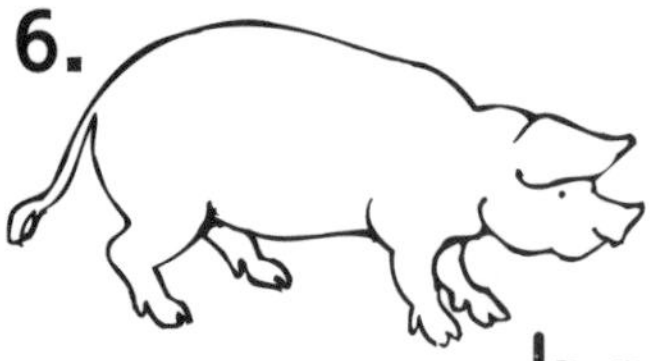

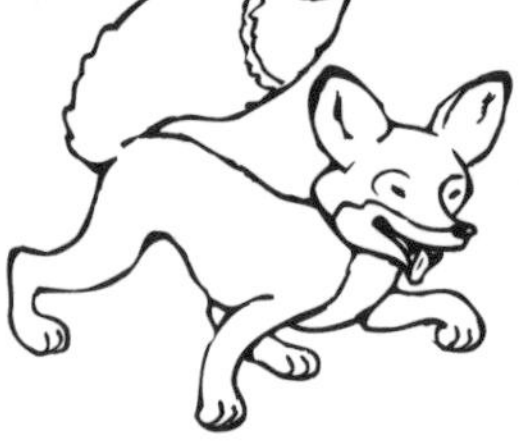

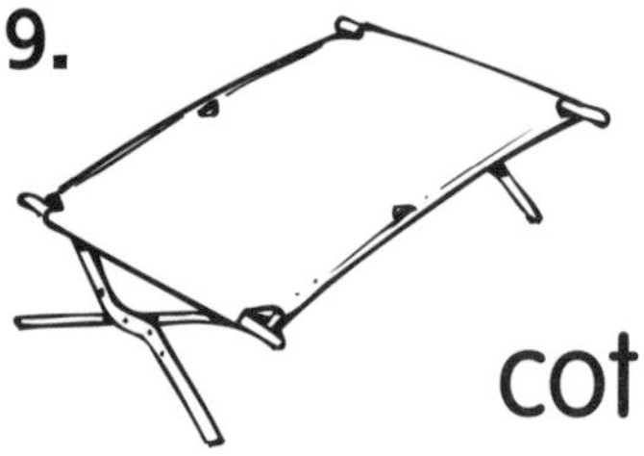

**Review and assessment of short o words**

Name _____

Listen for the **short a, i,** or **o** sound.
Write the correct vowel on the line
to complete the word.

# Tap, Tip, or Top?

tip
i

top
o

tap
a

| | | |
|---|---|---|
| **1.** t o p | **2.** l___d | **3.** b___t |
| **4.** f___x | **5.** h___m | **6.** b___b |
| **7.** p___t | **8.** s___x | **9.** f___n |

**Distinguishing among short a, short i, and short o sounds**

Name _____

Circle the picture if you hear the **short e** sound.

Ee
red
hen

**Get the red hen.**

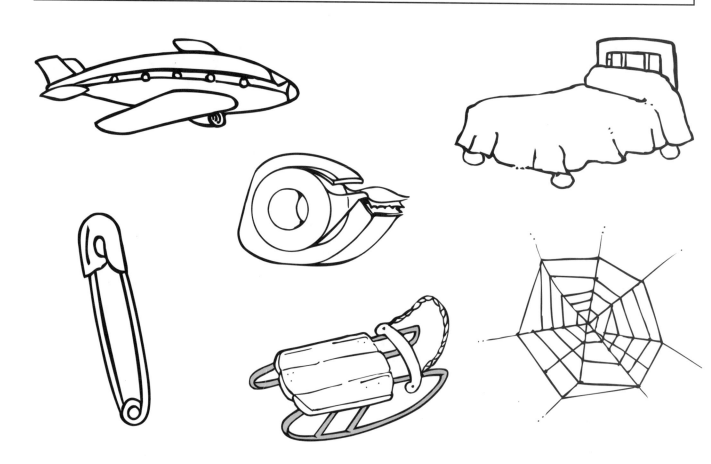

**To the Teacher:** Review the picture names with students.
(jet, bed, tape, pin, sled, web)

**Recognizing the short e sound /ĕ/**

   Basic Phonics Skills, Level B • EMC 3319 • ©2004 by Evan-Moor Corp.

Name _____

Say the sound each letter stands for.
Follow the arrow to blend the sounds.
Draw a line from the word to the picture it names.

# Say It

1. e g g

2. m e n

3. w e b

4. h e n

5. w e t

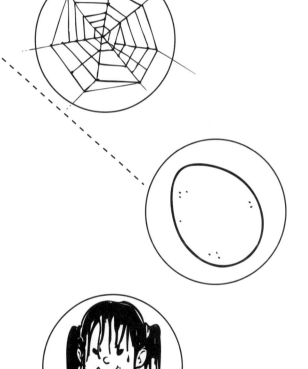

**Blending and matching words with the short e sound /ĕ/**

Name _____

Say the name of the picture.
Unscramble the letters.
Write the word.

# Unscramble It

1. 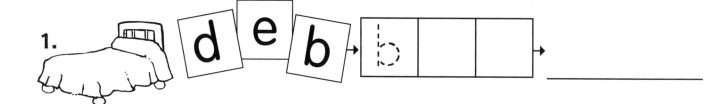 _____

2. 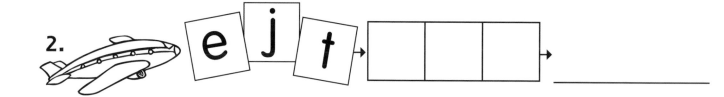 _____

3. 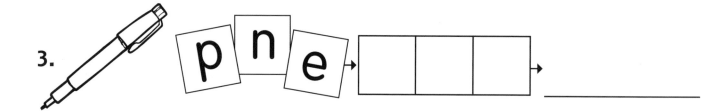 _____

4. 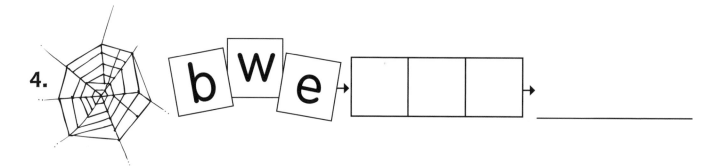 _____

5. 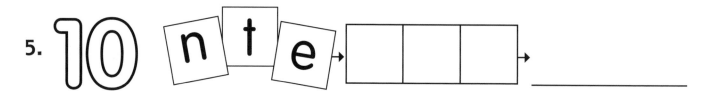 _____

**Phonics Fact!** Words that follow the CVC pattern have a short vowel.

**Blending and writing words with the short e sound /ĕ/**

Basic Phonics Skills, Level B • EMC 3319 • ©2004 by Evan-Moor Corp.

Name _____

Say the name of the picture.
Find the letters. Write the word.

| e | b | m | n | p | t | v | w |

1.   m | | | → _____

2.   | | | → _____

3.   | | | → _____

4.   | | | → _____

5. 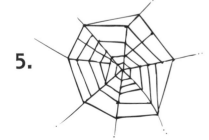  | | | → _____

**Blending and writing words with the short e sound /ĕ/**

Find the correct word in the word box.
Write the word on the lines.

# Match It Up

| egg | vet | hen |
|-----|-----|-----|
| wet | leg | jet |

**1.**

h e n

**2.**

\_ \_ \_

**3.**

\_ \_ \_

**4.**

\_ \_ \_

**5.**

\_ \_ \_

**6.**

\_ \_ \_

**Writing words with the short e sound /ĕ/**

Name _____

Listen to the beginning, middle, and ending sounds.
Write the word on the line.

# The Web

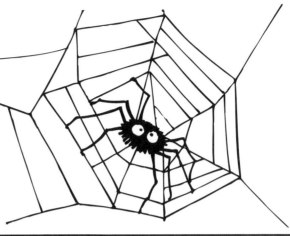

P**e**t is on the w**e**b.

| 1. | 2. | 3. |
|---|---|---|

m e n

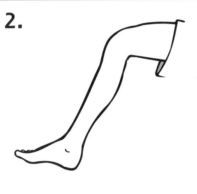

___ ___ ___

___ ___ ___

___ ___ ___

| 4. | 5. | 6. |
|---|---|---|

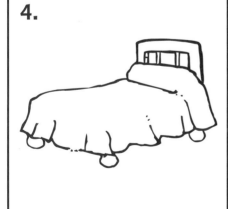

___ ___ ___

___ ___ ___

___ ___ ___

Name _____

Fill in the circle beside the word that best completes the sentence.
Write the word on the line.

1. Ben is on the _____.

    ○ fed    ○ get    ○ bed

2. Yes, Jen is _____.

    ○ pet    ○ wet    ○ web

3. My pet can _____.

    ○ bed    ○ fed    ○ beg

4. The hen is in the _____.

    ○ net    ○ pet    ○ pen

**Writing short e words to complete sentences**

Basic Phonics Skills, Level B • EMC 3319 • ©2004 by Evan-Moor Corp.

Name _____

Put the words in the correct order.
Write the sentence on the line.

# Get Your Pencil!

**Remember –** Every sentence begins with a capital letter.
Put a period (**.**) at the end.

| | |
|---|---|
| **1.** | has Ken a net<br><br>Ken _____ |
| **2.** | by jet a men the met<br><br>_____ |
| **3.** | hen has Jen a pet<br><br>_____ |
| **4.** | is my wet leg<br><br>_____ |

Writing sentences with short e words

Name _____

Read each sentence. Draw a line to match the sentence to the correct picture.

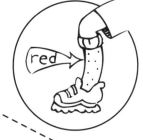

1. Ted's pet is wet.

2. The pet met the vet.

3. Ned's leg is red.

4. Get in the bed.

5. Get the pet in the net.

6. The next jet went.

**Reading short e words**

Basic Phonics Skills, Level B • EMC 3319 • ©2004 by Evan-Moor Corp.

Name _____

Cut out the pictures.
Listen for the vowel sounds.
Glue the pictures by the jet or the hot dog.

# Listen for the Vowels

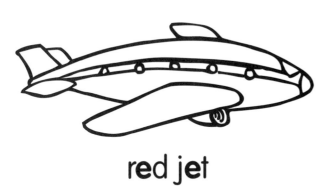

**re**d j**e**t

| | |
|---|---|
| glue | glue |
| glue | glue |

h**o**t d**o**g

| | |
|---|---|
| glue | glue |
| glue | glue |

**Identifying short e and short o words**

Name _____

Circle the word that names the picture.

My p**e**t is w**e**t.

| | | |
|---|---|---|
| **1.** get ~~pet~~ peg | **2.** pen pet hen | **3.** wet fed web |
| **4.** bed led den | **5.** met net men | **6.** set jet pen |
| **7.** peg red leg | **8.** ten wet jet | **9.** get vet yes |

**Review and assessment of short e words**

Basic Phonics Skills, Level B • EMC 3319 • ©2004 by Evan-Moor Corp.

Name _____

Say the name of the pictures.
Write the correct letter **a, i, o,** or **e** on the line to complete the word.

1.

h__t

2.

b__d

3.
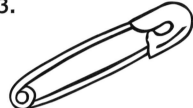
p__n

4.

c__t

5.
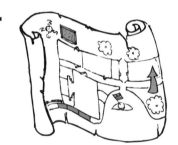
m__p

6.

l__g

7.

m__n

8.

d__g

9.

j__t

**Distinguishing between short a, short i, short o, and short e sounds**

Name _____

Circle the picture if you hear the **short u** sound.

# The Sun

**Uu**
sun

The s**u**n is **u**p.

**To the Teacher:** Review the picture names with students.
(cup, drum, rug, top, van, gum)

**Recognizing the short u sound /ŭ/**

Basic Phonics Skills, Level B • EMC 3319 • ©2004 by Evan-Moor Corp.

Name _____

Say the sound each letter stands for.
Follow the arrow to blend the sounds.
Draw a line from the word to the picture it names.

# Say It

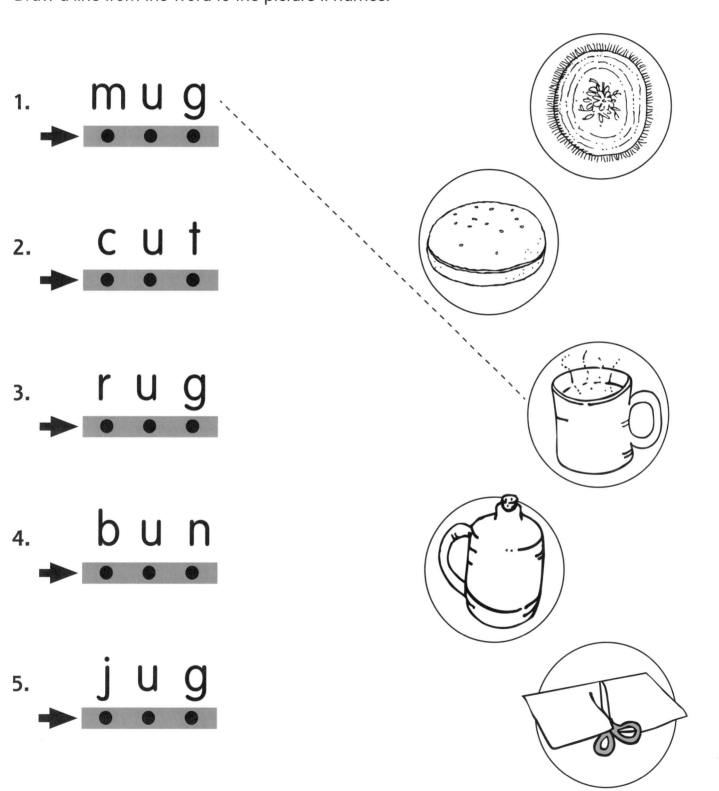

1. m u g

2. c u t

3. r u g

4. b u n

5. j u g

**Blending and matching words with the short u sound /ŭ/**

Name _____

Say the name of the picture.
Unscramble the letters.
Write the word.

# Unscramble It

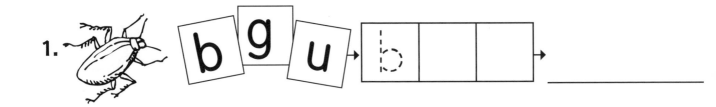

1.

b  g  u  →  b  ☐  ☐  →  _____

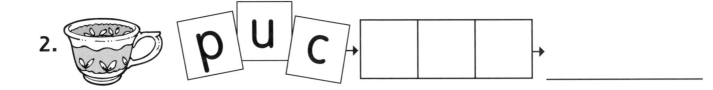

2.

p  u  c  →  ☐  ☐  ☐  →  _____

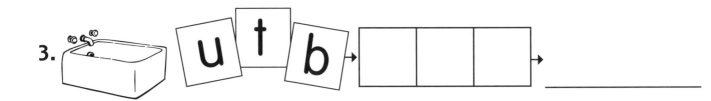

3.

u  t  b  →  ☐  ☐  ☐  →  _____

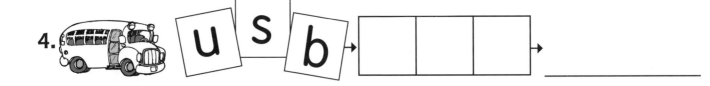

4.

u  s  b  →  ☐  ☐  ☐  →  _____

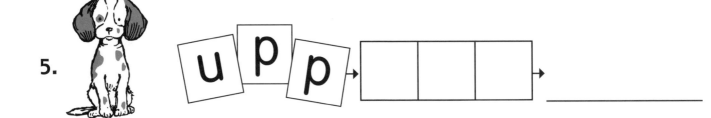

5.

u  p  p  →  ☐  ☐  ☐  →  _____

**Phonics Fact!** Words that follow the CVC pattern have a short vowel.

**Blending and writing words with the short u sound /ŭ/**

Basic Phonics Skills, Level B • EMC 3319 • ©2004 by Evan-Moor Corp.

Name _____

Say the name of the picture.
Find the letters.
Write the word.

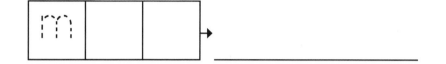

u  b  g  m  n  s  t

1. | m |   |   | → _____

2. |   |   |   | → _____

3. |   |   |   | → _____

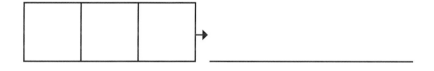

4. |   |   |   | → _____

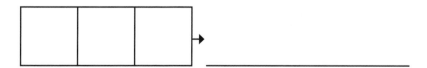

5. |   |   |   | → _____

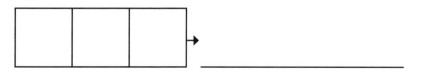

**Blending and writing words with the short u sound /ŭ/**

Find the correct word in the word box.
Write the word on the lines.

# Match It Up

| cub | hug | run |
|-----|-----|-----|
| bug | sun | rug |

**1.**

c u b

**2.**

— — —

**3.**

— — —

**4.**

— — —

**5.**

— — —

**6.**

— — —

**Writing words with the short u sound /ŭ/**

Name _____

Listen to the beginning, middle, and ending sounds. Write the word on the line.

# Hug It

**1.**

h u t

**2.**

_ _ _

**3.**

_ _ _

**4.**

_ _ _

**5.**

_ _ _

**6.**

_ _ _

**Writing words with the short u sound /ŭ/**

**Short Vowel Sounds** 193

Name _____

Fill in the circle beside the word that best completes the sentence. Write the word on the line.

# Don't Hug a Skunk!

1.
You must not _____ a skunk.

    ○ hug    ○ fun    ○ tub

2.
Bud gets on the _____.

    ○ bun    ○ hum    ○ bus

3.
The mud is on the _____.

    ○ pup    ○ bug    ○ duck

4.
I hung the _____ in the sun.

    ○ jug    ○ rug    ○ rut

Writing short u words to complete sentences

    Basic Phonics Skills, Level B • EMC 3319 • ©2004 by Evan-Moor Corp.

Name _____

Put the words in the correct order.
Write the sentence on the line.
Begin each sentence with a capital letter.

# Sun's Up!

Remember—A sentence begins with a capital letter.
It usually ends with a period (.).

| 1. | in is bug the a cup |
| --- | --- |
| | The _____ |

| 2. | sun is up the |
| --- | --- |
| | _____ |

| 3. | dug a cub up the nut |
| --- | --- |
| | _____ |

| 4. | up cut the Bud rug |
| --- | --- |
| | _____ |

Writing sentences with short u words

Name _____

Read each sentence.
Circle each word that has a **short u** sound.
Draw a line to match the sentence to the correct picture.

1. Russ jumps on the rug.

2. A bug runs up a jug.

3. The cub is in the mud.

4. Bud has fun in the tub.

5. Pug dug in the sun.

6. It is fun to hug a pup.

**Reading short u words**

Name _____

Cut out the pictures. Listen for the vowel sounds.
Glue the pictures by the sun or the hens.

# Listen for the Vowels

**fun sun**

| glue | glue |
|------|------|
| glue | glue |

**ten hens**

| glue | glue |
|------|------|
| glue | glue |

**Identifying short u and short e words**

Name _____

Circle the word that names the picture.

h**u**mmmm m m m m m

**1.**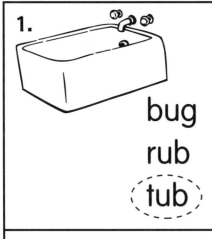

bug
rub
(tub)

**2.**

mud
mug
jug

**3.**

cub
bug
cut

**4.**

cup
pup
bud

**5.**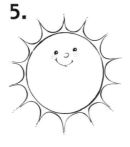

fun
hum
sun

**6.**

bus
sub
cub

**7.**

bun
hug
nut

**8.**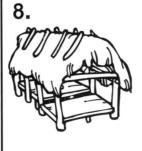

hut
rug
tug

**9.**

sum
rug
gum

**Review and assessment of short u words**

Basic Phonics Skills, Level B • EMC 3319 • ©2004 by Evan-Moor Corp.

Name _____

Say the name of each picture.
Listen for the short vowel sound.
Write the correct letter **a, i, o, e,** or **u**
on the line to complete the word.

# Bag, Big, Bog, Beg, or Bug?

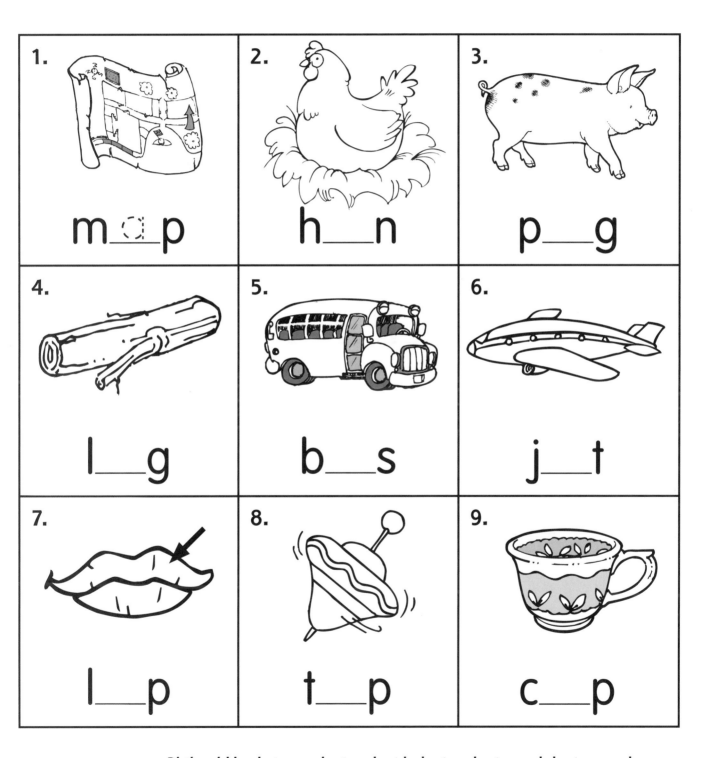

1. m a p

2. h__n

3. p__g

4. l__g

5. b__s

6. j__t

7. l__p

8. t__p

9. c__p

**Distinguishing between short a, short i, short o, short e, and short u sounds**

Name _____

Say the name of each picture.
Write 2 words beside the picture that have
the same vowel sound.

| bug | dog | pan | lid | net |
| hat | bib | bed | box | cup |

**1.** pan _____ _____

**2.** _____ _____

**3.** _____ _____

**4.** _____ _____

**5.** _____ _____

Review short a, short e, short i, short o, and short u sounds

# Plural and Inflectional Endings

Name _____

Add the letter **s** to make each word plural.

# More Than One

**Phonics Fact!** **Singular** means only one. **Plural** means more than one. To make a word say more than one, you sometimes add just the letter **s**.

1.     bed    bed_s__

2.     hat    hat___

3. 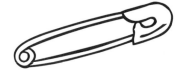    pin    pin___

4.     nut    nut___

5.     sub    sub___

Plural Endings: Adding –s

Name _____

Add the letters **es** to make each word plural.

# Still More Than One

| | | |
|---|---|---|
| 1. |  six | six⬭ ⬭ |
| 2. |  dress | dress____ __ |
| 3. |  dish | dish__ __ |
| 4. |  box | box__ __ |
| 5. | 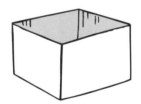 bus | bus__ __ |
| 6. |  kiss | kiss__ __ |

Plural Endings: Adding –es

Name _____

Add the correct ending **s** or **es** to each word to make it mean more than one.

# How Many?

| | | | |
|---|---|---|---|
| 1. |  | pen | pen s ___ |
| 2. | 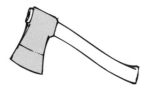 | ax | ax___ ___ |
| 3. |  | log | log___ ___ |
| 4. |  | can | can___ ___ |
| 5. |  | bush | bush___ ___ |
| 6. |  | bus | bus___ ___ |

Plural Endings: Adding –s or –es

Basic Phonics Skills, Level B • EMC 3319 • ©2004 by Evan-Moor Corp.

Name _____

Add **s** or **es** to the words.

# Add an Ending

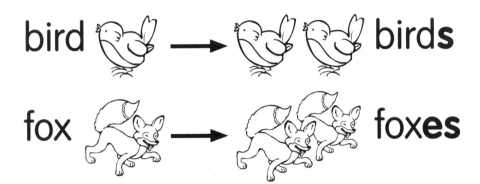

bird → birds

fox → foxes

| | | |
|---|---|---|
| **1.** bat  bats | **2.** bus  | **3.** can  |
| **4.** box  | **5.** dress  | **6.** bush  |

**Plural Endings: Writing plural words**

Name _____

Circle the word that best completes the sentence.
Write the word on the line.

# Cat or Cats?

1.  My _____ is in its bed.

   (cat)    cats

2.  The _____ are by the pan.

   dish    dishes

3.  Linn has lots of _____.

   egg    eggs

4.  Here is a _____ for you.

   jug    jugs

5.  Mom gave me a _____.

   kisses    kiss

Plural Endings: Writing plural words to complete sentences

Basic Phonics Skills, Level B • EMC 3319 • ©2004 by Evan-Moor Corp.

Name _____

# First Base

Read each word. Underline the base word. Write the word on the line.

| | | |
|---|---|---|
| 1. **balls** | <u>ball</u> |  |
| 2. **wishes** | _____ |  |
| 3. **passes** | _____ |  |
| 4. **hits** | _____ |  |
| 5. **buses** | _____ |  |

**Identifying the base word**

Name _____

**Phonics Fact!**

A letter or letters that are added to the end of a base word is called a **suffix**.
The plural endings **–s** and **–es** are suffixes.
Two more suffixes are **–ed** and **–ing**.

Read each base word. Write the new words on the lines.

| Base Word | Add –ed | Add –ing |
|-----------|---------|----------|
| jump | jumped | _____ |
| climb | _____ | _____ |
| look | _____ | _____ |
| play | _____ | _____ |
| walk | _____ | _____ |
| wash | _____ | _____ |

**Adding the endings –ed and –ing to words**

Basic Phonics Skills, Level B • EMC 3319 • ©2004 by Evan-Moor Corp.

Name _____

Circle the word that best completes the sentence.
Write the word on the line.

# Buzz!

1. The bee _____ by my ear.

   buzzing    buzzed

2. Nan is _____ her dad.

   helping    helped

3. Max _____ the ball to Jan.

   tossing    tossed

4. Kim is _____ over
   the box.

   jumping    jumped

Writing words with –ed and –ing to complete sentences

Name _____

Circle the word that best goes with the picture.
Underline the base word.

# Review
## Base Words
## with Endings

1. boxes    boxing

2. spilled    spills

3. ducks    ducked

4. dressing    dresses

5. brushed    brushing

6. nailed    nails

# Word Families

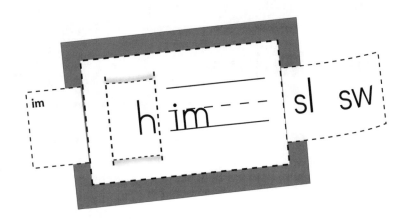

# Word Family Sliders

## Materials

- reproducible sheets on pages 213, 216, 219, 222, 225, 228, 231
- 3 ½" x 5" (9 x 13 cm) construction paper cards
- craft knife
- glue
- scissors

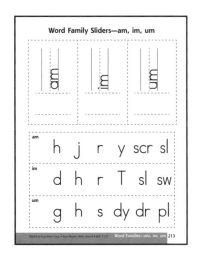

## Steps to Follow

1. Reproduce the word family slider sheets. Select the word families you wish to practice, and cut on the dotted lines.

2. Glue the word family holder to the construction paper.

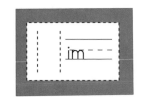

3. Use a craft knife to slit along the dotted lines on the word family holders.

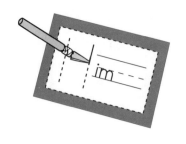

4. Insert the correct letter strip.

5. Demonstrate to students how to pull the strip through the holder.

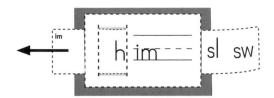

Basic Phonics Skills, Level B • EMC 3319 • ©2004 by Evan-Moor Corp.

# Word Family Sliders—am, im, um

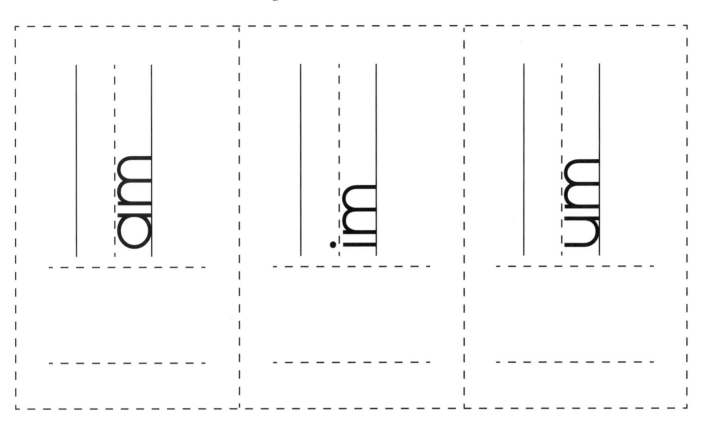

**am**

h  j  r  y  scr  sl

**im**

d  h  r  T  sl  sw

**um**

g  h  s  dy  dr  pl

Name _____

Cut and paste to complete each word.

# Cut & Paste

1. h glue

2. dr glue

3. cl glue

4. j glue

5. g glue

6. sw glue

| am | im | um | am | im | um |

**Word Families—am, im, um**   Basic Phonics Skills, Level B • EMC 3319 • ©2004 by Evan-Moor Corp.

Name  _____

Circle the word that names the picture.
Write a new word.

**1.**

Tim
(rim)
slim

Write a new word.

him

**2.**

dim
trim
Jim

Write a new word.

_____

**3.**

Sam
jam
ram

Write a new word.

_____

**4.**

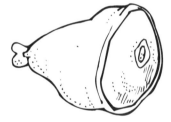

yam
ham
dam

Write a new word.

_____

**5.**

plum
gum
drum

Write a new word.

_____

**6.**

bum
yum
hum

Write a new word.

_____

# Word Family Sliders—ip, ap, op

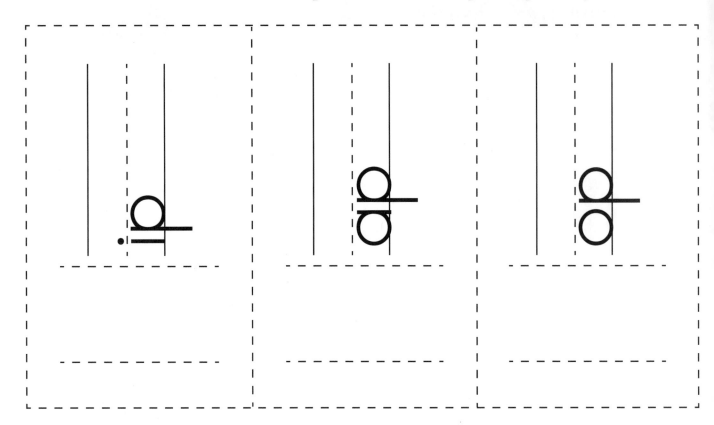

**ip**

d   r   s   z   dr   sh

**ap**

c   m   n   t   cl   wr

**op**

h   m   p   t   dr   st

Name _____

Cut and paste to complete each word.

# Cut & Paste

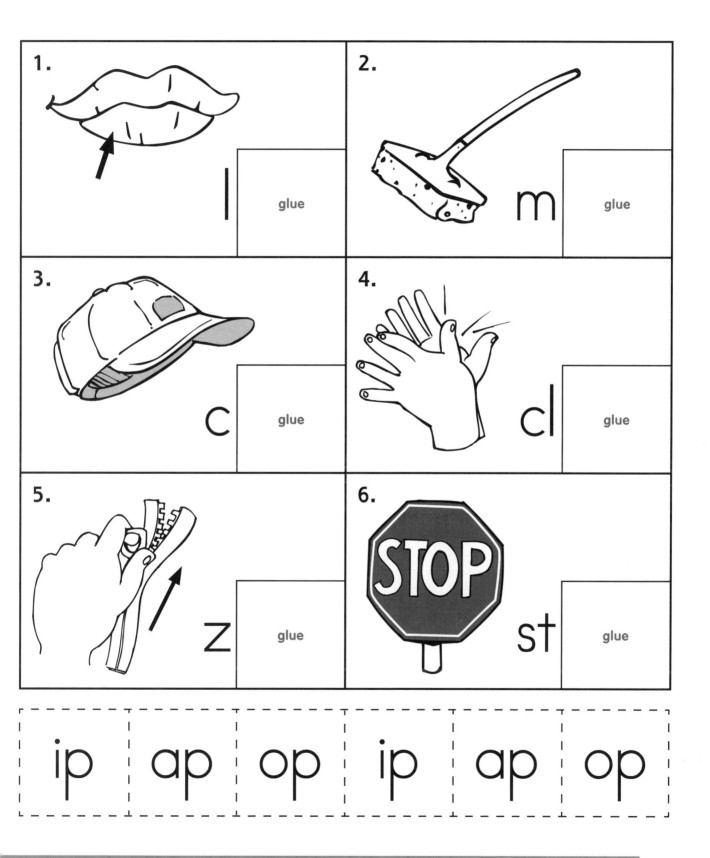

1. l [glue]

2. m [glue]

3. c [glue]

4. cl [glue]

5. z [glue]

6. st [glue]

ip | ap | op | ip | ap | op

Name _____

Circle the word that names the picture.
Write a new word.

**1.**

lip
(sip)
rip

Write a new word.

tip

**2.**

stop
hop
mop

Write a new word.

_____

**3.**
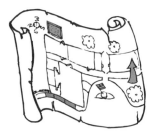
lap
map
clap

Write a new word.

_____

**4.**

zip
hip
drip

Write a new word.

_____

**5.**

cap
slap
nap

Write a new word.

_____

**6.**

shop
top
pop

Write a new word.

_____

Basic Phonics Skills, Level B • EMC 3319 • ©2004 by Evan-Moor Corp.

# Word Family Sliders—at, et, it

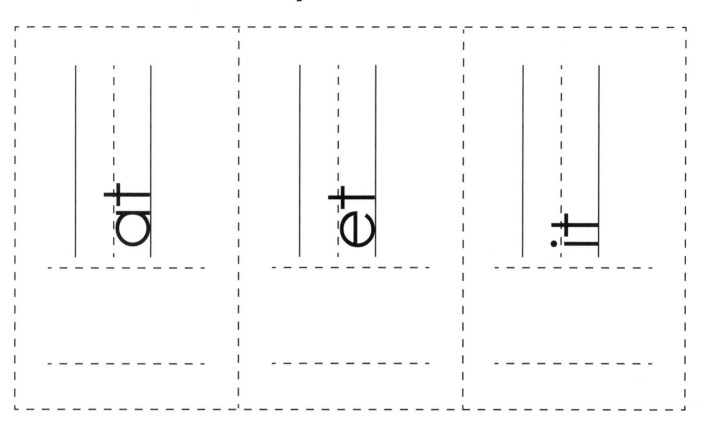

**at**

b  c  h  m  fl  ch

**et**

g  j  m  n  p  w

**it**

b  f  h  p  s  sl

Name _____

Cut and paste to complete each word.

# Cut & Paste

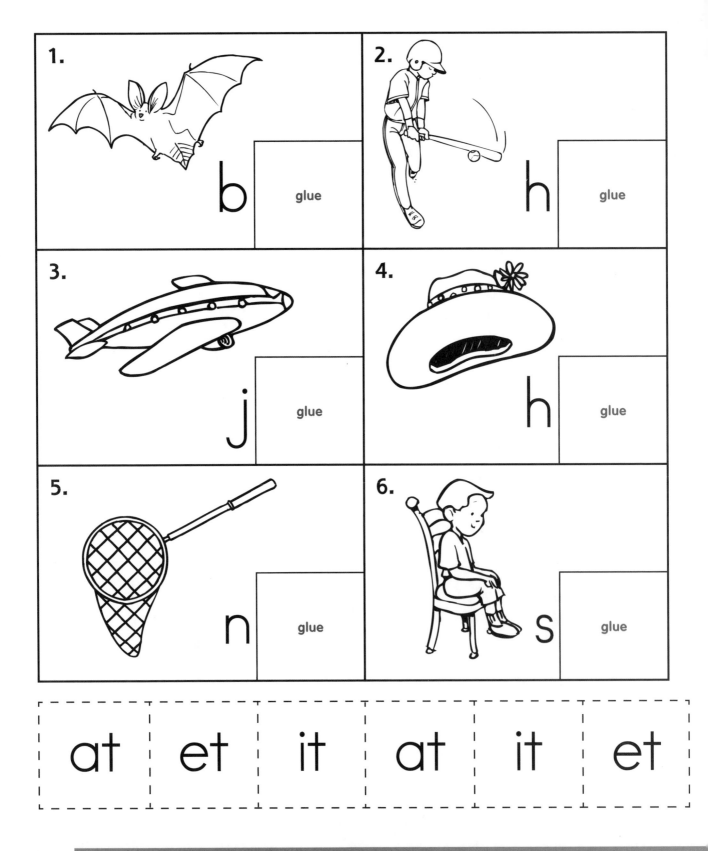

1. b [glue]

2. h [glue]

3. j [glue]

4. h [glue]

5. n [glue]

6. s [glue]

at | et | it | at | it | et

 Basic Phonics Skills, Level B • EMC 3319 • ©2004 by Evan-Moor Corp.

Name _____

Circle the word that names the picture.
Write a new word.

**1.**

hat

(cat)

fat

Write a new word.

bat

**2.**

jet

set

wet

Write a new word.

_____

**3.**

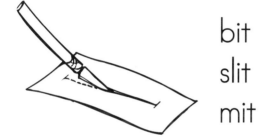

bit

slit

mit

Write a new word.

_____

**4.**

get

vet

fret

Write a new word.

_____

**5.**

flat

bat

rat

Write a new word.

_____

**6.**

fit

hit

flit

Write a new word.

_____

# Word Family Sliders—ad, ed, od

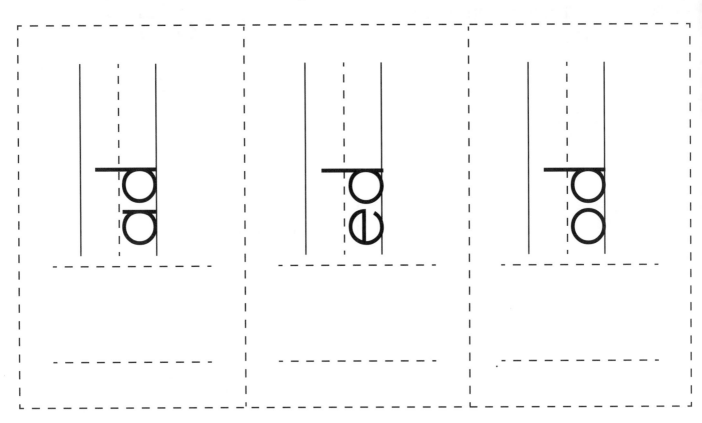

**ad**

b d l m s gl

**ed**

b f r w fl sl

**od**

c n p r s pl

Basic Phonics Skills, Level B • EMC 3319 • ©2004 by Evan-Moor Corp.

Name _____

Cut and paste to complete each word.

# Cut & Paste

Name _____

Circle the word that names the picture.
Write a new word.

**1.**

mad
sad
had

Write a new word.

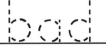

**2.**

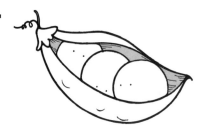

cod
pod
nod

Write a new word.

_____

**3.**

fed
bed
wed

Write a new word.

_____

**4.**

bad
dad
glad

Write a new word.

_____

**5.**

led
fled
red

Write a new word.

_____

**6.**

sod
rod
cod

Write a new word.

_____

# Word Family Sliders—an, in, un

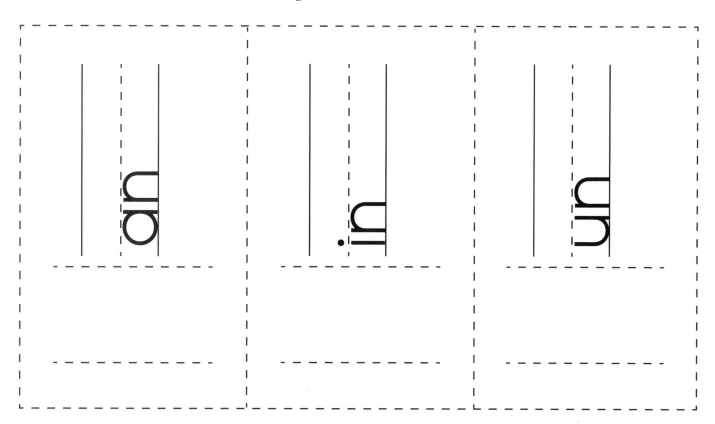

an

c   f   m   p   v   pl

in

b   f   p   w   gr   tw

un

b   f   g   r   s   sp

Name _____

Cut and paste to complete each word.

# Cut & Paste

1. Spaghetti Curlys — c [glue]

2. (sun) s [glue]

3. (safety pin) p [glue]

4. (running boy) r [glue]

5. (boy with trophy) w [glue]

6. (bun) b [glue]

an | in | un | an | in | un

Name _____

Circle the word that names the picture.
Write a new word.

**1.**

(fan)
can
pan

Write a new word.

tan

**2.**

pin
fin
bin

Write a new word.

_____

**3.**

fun
bun
sun

Write a new word.

_____

**4.**

tin
kin
twin

Write a new word.

_____

**5.**

ban
man
ran

Write a new word.

_____

**6.**

spun
run
pun

Write a new word.

_____

# Word Family Sliders—ig, og, ug

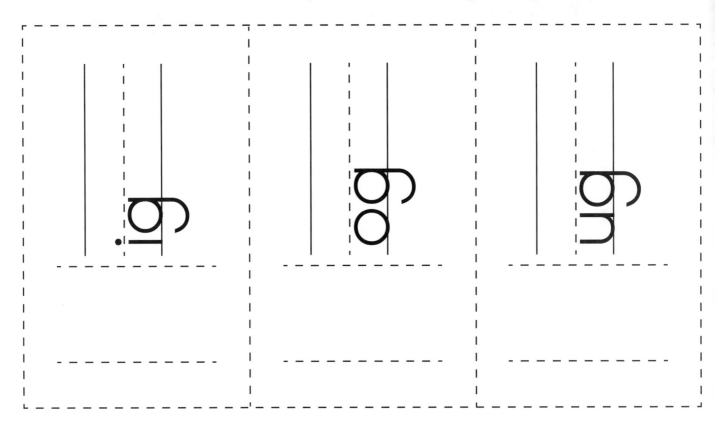

ig

b f j p w tw

og

d f h l fr sm

ug

b d h m r sl

Name _____

Cut and paste to complete each word.

# Cut & Paste

1. p ⬚ glue

2. l ⬚ glue

3. d ⬚ glue

4. m ⬚ glue

5. w ⬚ glue

6. r ⬚ glue

ig | og | ug | ig | og | ug

Name _____

Circle the word that names the picture.
Write a new word.

**1.**

(big)
fig
jig

Write a new word.

wig

**2.**

bug
jug
mug

Write a new word.

_____

**3.**

fog
bog
dog

Write a new word.

_____

**4.**

pig
twig
dig

Write a new word.

_____

**5.**

jog
frog
dog

Write a new word.

_____

**6.**

hug
dug
rug

Write a new word.

_____

Basic Phonics Skills, Level B • EMC 3319 • ©2004 by Evan-Moor Corp.

# Word Family Sliders—ack, eck, ick

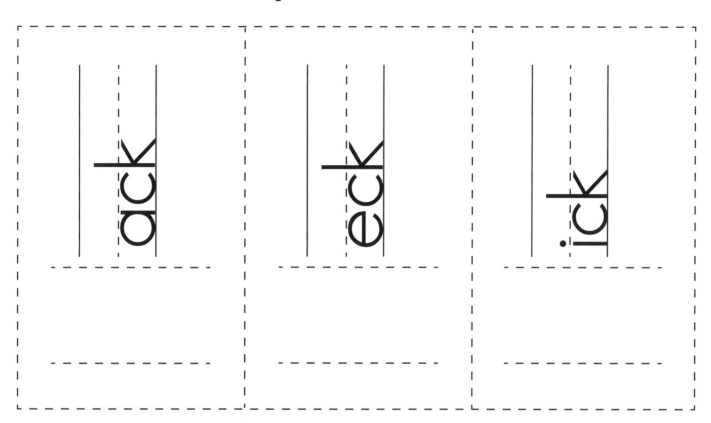

**ack**

qu   r   s   bl   cr   st

**eck**

d   n   p   sp   wr

**ick**

k   l   p   s   t   st

Name _____

Cut and paste to complete each word.

# Cut & Paste

1.

s [glue]

2. tock

t [glue]

3.

n [glue]

4.

s [glue]

5.

cr [glue]

6.

sp [glue]

| ack | eck | ick | ack | eck | ick |

Basic Phonics Skills, Level B • EMC 3319 • ©2004 by Evan-Moor Corp.

Name _____

Circle the word that names the picture.
Write a new word.

**1.**

(quack)
back
Jack

Write a new word.

rack

**2.**

speck
peck
neck

Write a new word.

_____

**3.**

wreck
neck
deck

Write a new word.

_____

**4.**

kick
sick
nick

Write a new word.

_____

**5.**

pack
flack
black

Write a new word.

_____

**6.**

lick
stick
pick

Write a new word.

_____

Name _____

Write the word that names the picture.
Change the first letter and make a new word.

# Word Families Review

| dog | lick | fan | bed | cat | sack | hop | run | hit |

**1.**    c a t     r a t

**2.**

**3.**

**4.**

**5.**

**6.**

**7.**

**8.**

**9.**

Basic Phonics Skills, Level B • EMC 3319 • ©2004 by Evan-Moor Corp.

# Word Family Tree

## Materials

- page 236, reproduced for each student
- crayons or marking pens
- pencil

## Steps to Follow

1. Write on the chalkboard or overhead the sound chunk for which you will build a word family.
2. Have students write the "chunk" on the tree's trunk.
3. Challenge students to fill the treetop with words belonging to that word family.
4. Color the tree and add a background.
5. Repeat with other chunks as those sounds are studied.

## Extensions

- After making a word family tree for a number of word chunks, bind each student's pages together to create a "word family album." Add a decorative cover.
- Create a class word family album. Give each student or group of students specific chunks to use.
- Create a "Forest of Word Families" bulletin board by posting word family trees.

Name _____

bug

tug

hug

mug

dug

jug

ug

Basic Phonics Skills, Level B • EMC 3319 • ©2004 by Evan-Moor Corp.

# Short Vowel Practice
# Little Phonics Readers

**BASIC** Phonics Skills

# How to Construct the Little Phonics Readers

## Materials

- story forms, reproduced for each student
- scissors
- stapler

## Steps to Follow

1. Copy a book for each student.
2. Cut out the pages on the dotted lines.
3. Fold the pages on the solid lines.
4. Place pages 2, 3, 4, and 5 inside the front cover section.

5. Fit the book into the stapler so that you can staple on the spine.

Basic Phonics Skills, Level B • EMC 3319 • ©2004 by Evan-Moor Corp.

1

Dad can nap.

—short a

# Dad and the Ant

fold 2

fold 1

6

Dad's mad!

Make a Match

ant

bag

Dad

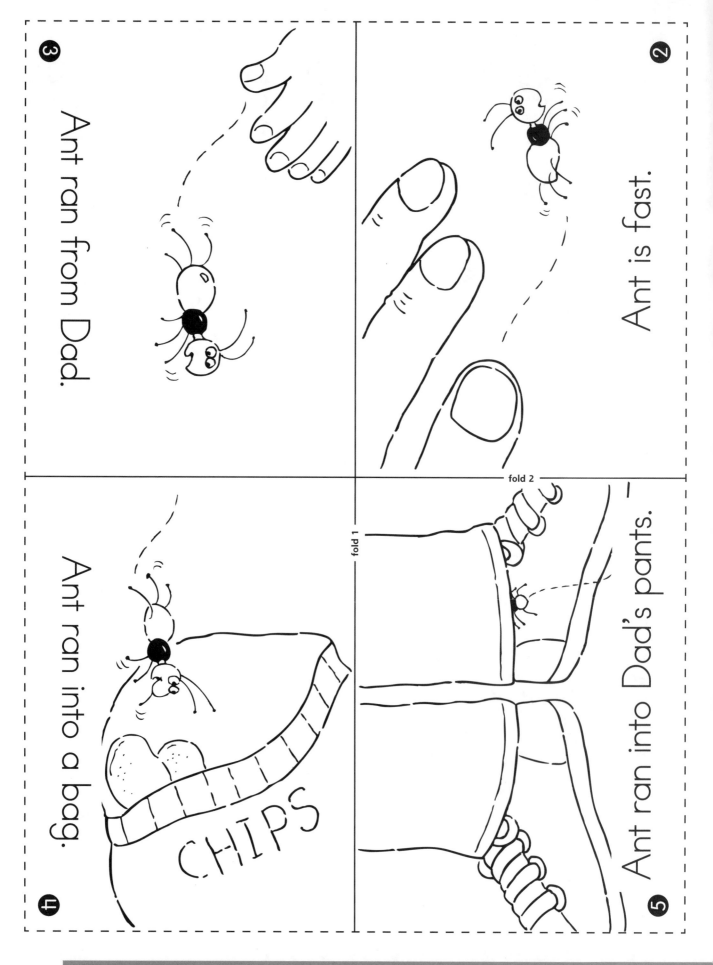

③ Ant ran from Dad.

② Ant is fast.

④ Ant ran into a bag.

CHIPS

⑤ Ant ran into Dad's pants.

fold 1

fold 2

**Little Phonics Readers**

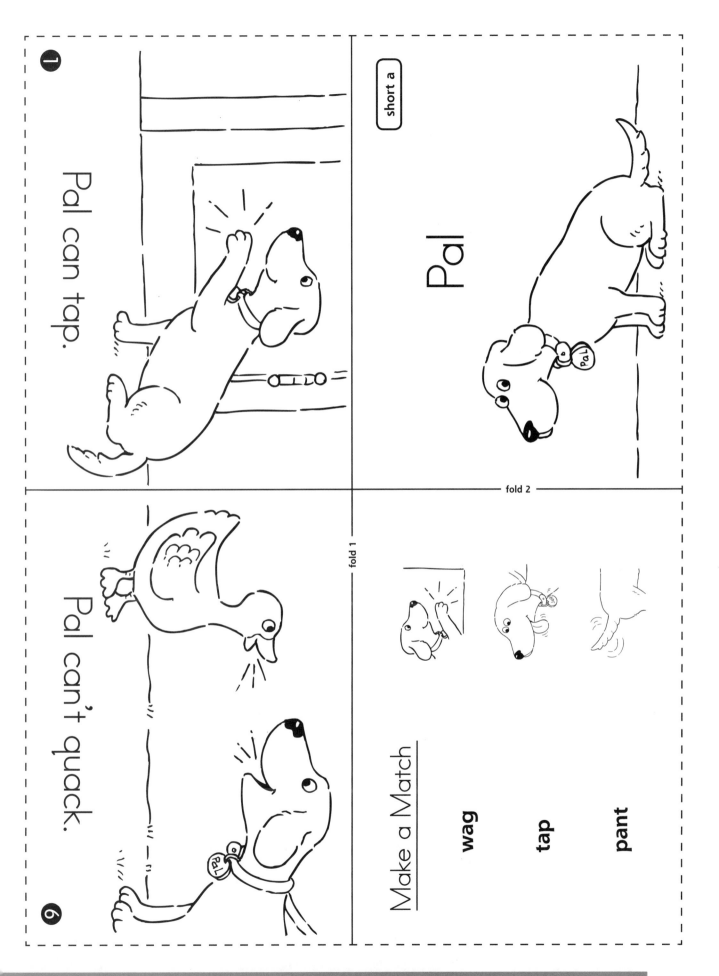

❶

Pal can tap.

Pal

fold 2

fold 1

❻

Pal can't quack.

Make a Match

wag

tap

pant

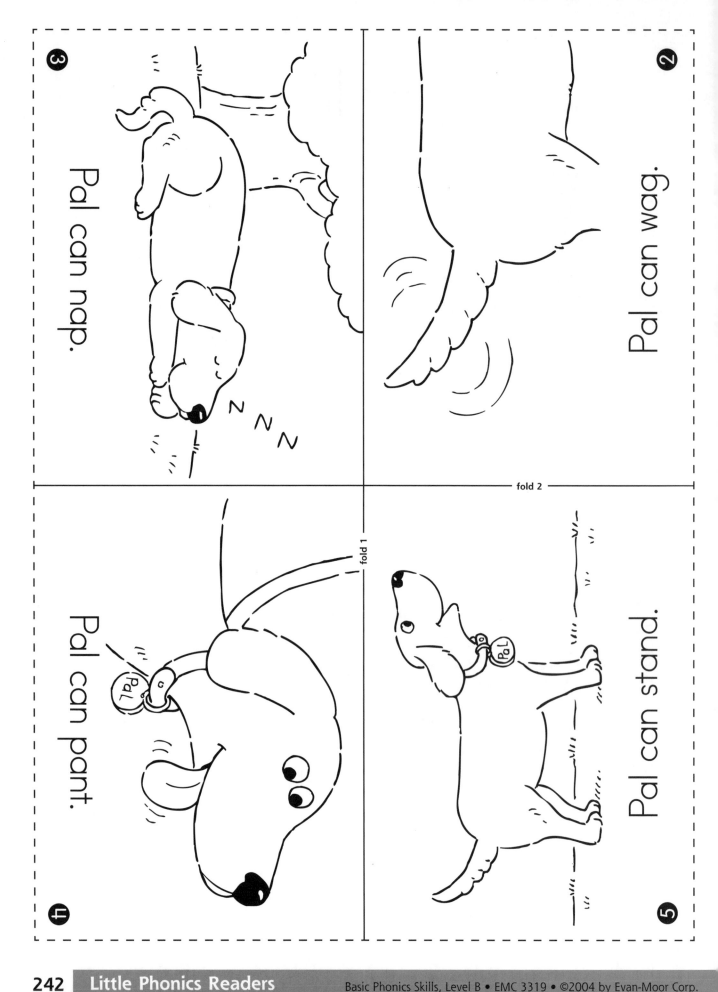

❸ Pal can nap.

❷ Pal can wag.

❹ Pal can pant.

❺ Pal can stand.

fold 2

fold 1

**Little Phonics Readers**   Basic Phonics Skills, Level B • EMC 3319 • ©2004 by Evan-Moor Corp.

**1**

Did Tip dig?

short i

Tip

fold 2

fold 1

Make a Match

sit

dig

Tip did!

**9**

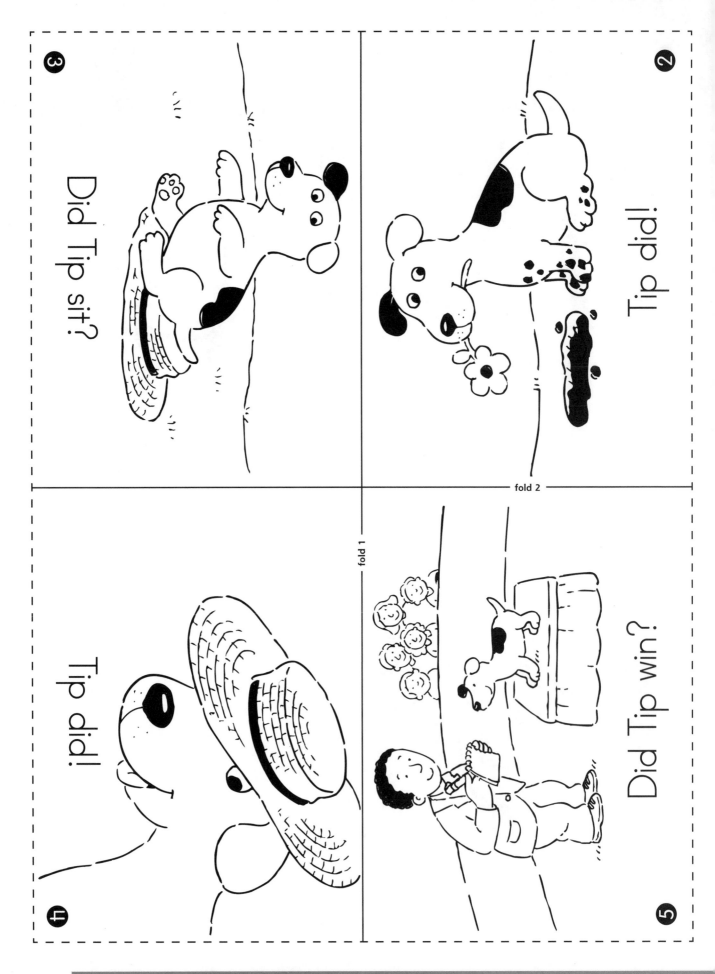

③ Did Tip sit?

② Tip did!

fold 2

fold 1

④ Tip did!

⑤ Did Tip win?

**Little Phonics Readers**    Basic Phonics Skills, Level B • EMC 3319 • ©2004 by Evan-Moor Corp.

1

Will Jill fit in?

short i

Will It Fit?

fold 2

fold 1

Hit six.

6

Make a Match

Sid

Jill

Liz

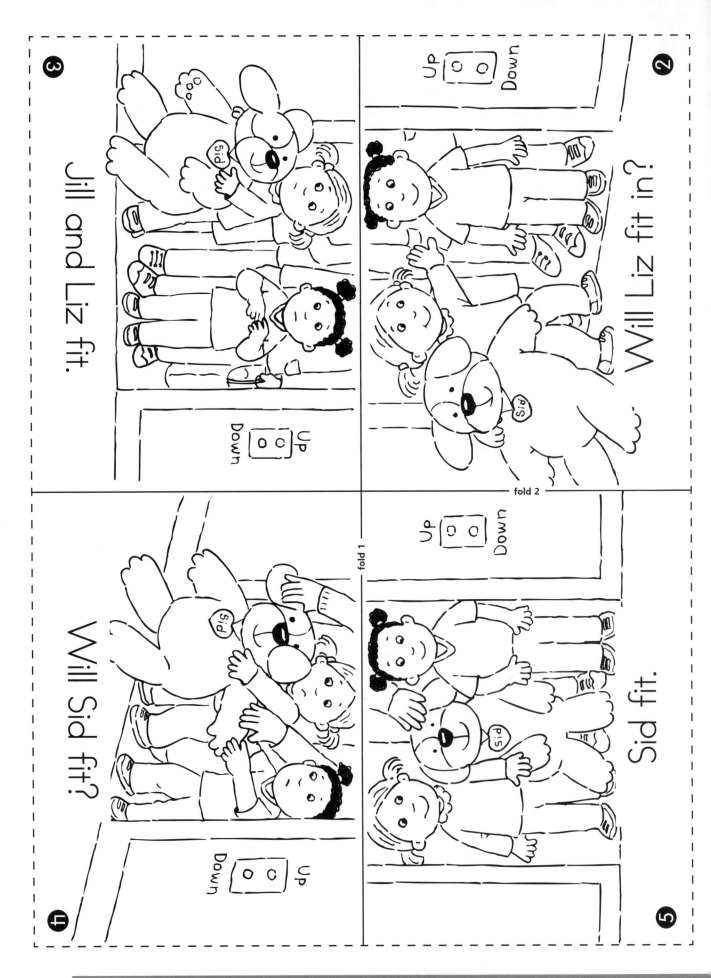

③ Jill and Liz fit.

② Will Liz fit in?

④ Will Sid fit?

⑤ Sid fit.

Basic Phonics Skills, Level B • EMC 3319 • ©2004 by Evan-Moor Corp.

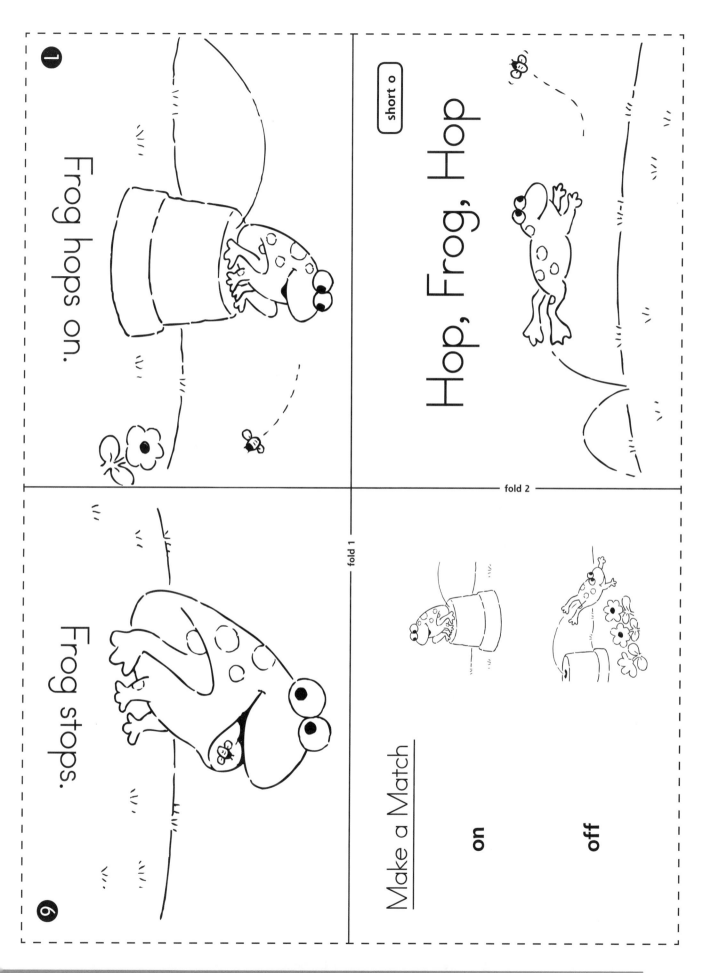

**1**

Frog hops on.

short o

# Hop, Frog, Hop

fold 2

fold 1

**6**

Frog stops.

<u>Make a Match</u>

on

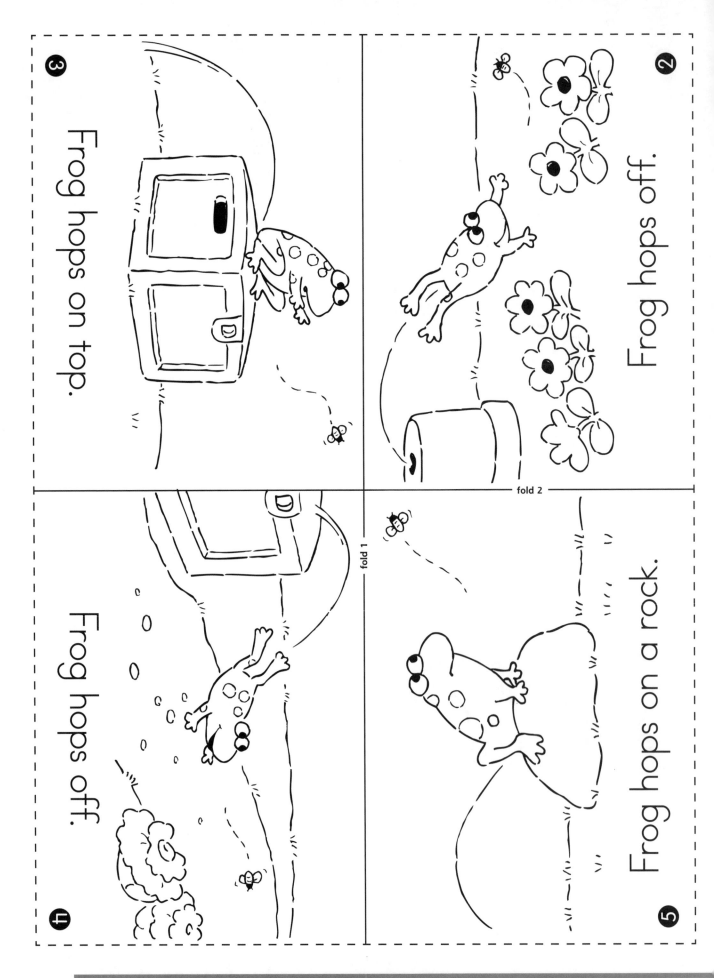

③ Frog hops on top.

② Frog hops off.

fold 2

fold 1

④ Frog hops off.

⑤ Frog hops on a rock.

Basic Phonics Skills, Level B • EMC 3319 • ©2004 by Evan-Moor Corp.

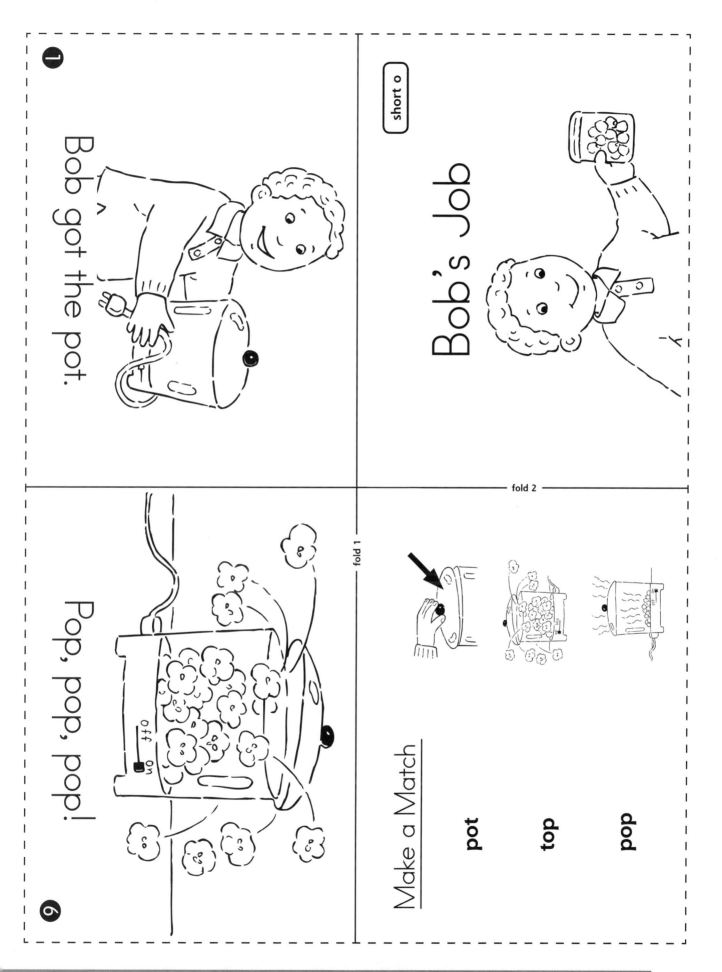

**1**

Bob got the pot.

short o

Bob's Job

fold 2

fold 1

Pop, pop, pop!

**6**

Make a Match

pot

top

pop

③ Pop on the top.

② The pot is not hot.

fold 2

fold 1

④ Off On

⑤ The pot is hot.

Basic Phonics Skills, Level B • EMC 3319 • ©2004 by Evan-Moor Corp.

**1** Ted and Ed went to help.

Let them rest. **6**

fold 1

fold 2

short e

Ted and Ed

Make a Match

**Ted**

**Ed**

❸ Ted and Ed help test.

❷ Ted and Ed get wet.

❹ Ted and Ed help sell.

❺ Ted and Ed went to bed.

fold 2

fold 1

 Basic Phonics Skills, Level B • EMC 3319 • ©2004 by Evan-Moor Corp.

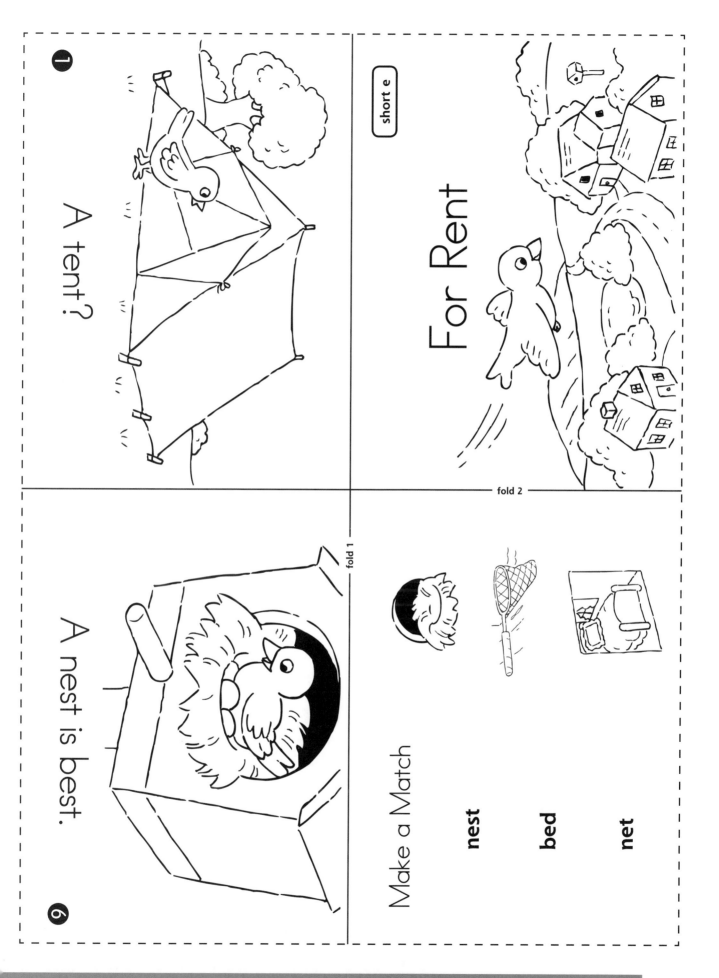

**1**

A tent?

short e

For Rent

fold 2

fold 1

A nest is best.

Make a Match

nest

bed

net

**6**

③ A bed?

② A net?

Too wet

fold 2

fold 1

④ A nest?

⑤ Yes, a nest!

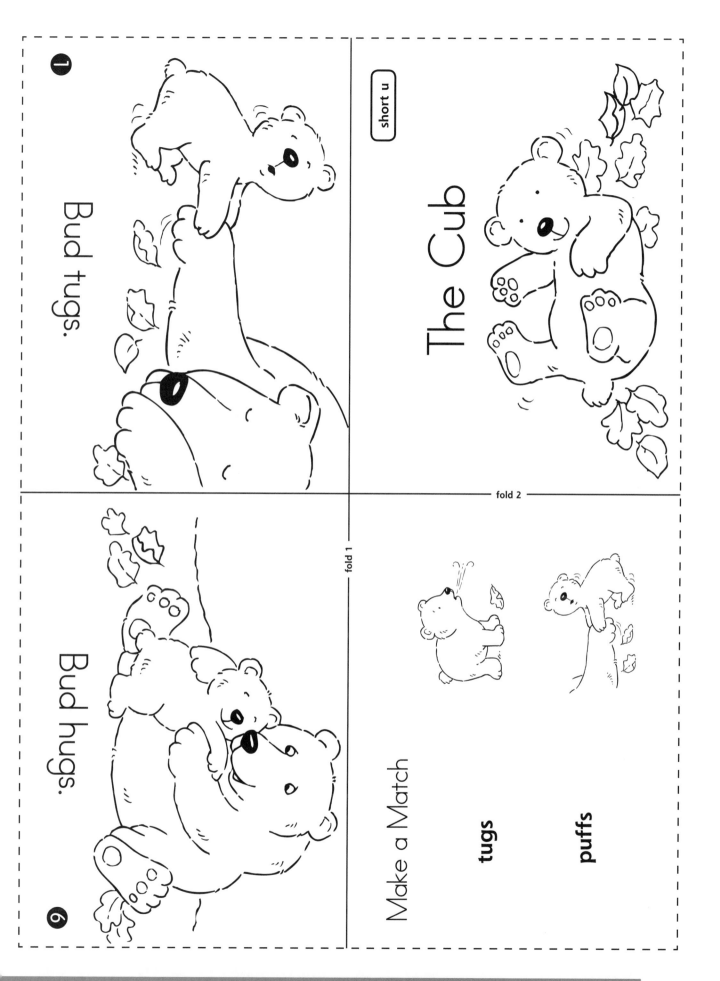

**1**

Bud tugs.

The Cub

fold 2

fold 1

Make a Match

tugs

puffs

Bud hugs.

**6**

Bud puffs.

③

Bud rubs.

②

Bud hums.

④

Bud runs.

⑤

fold 2

fold 1

 Basic Phonics Skills, Level B • EMC 3319 • ©2004 by Evan-Moor Corp.

Gus and Pup

**1**

Fun in the sun.

Rub-a-dub-dub.
Fun in the tub.

**6**

Make a Match

**sun**

**mud**

**Gus**

fold 2

fold 1

**3** Pup tugs Gus into the mud.

**2** Pup jumps into the mud.

**4** Pup runs to the tub.

**5** Gus runs into the tub.

fold 1

fold 2

 Basic Phonics Skills, Level B • EMC 3319 • ©2004 by Evan-Moor Corp.

**1**

Pam

—am family

# A Swimming Lesson

fold 2

fold 1

Make a Match

**Gram**

**Sam**

**Pam**

Gram swam.

**9**

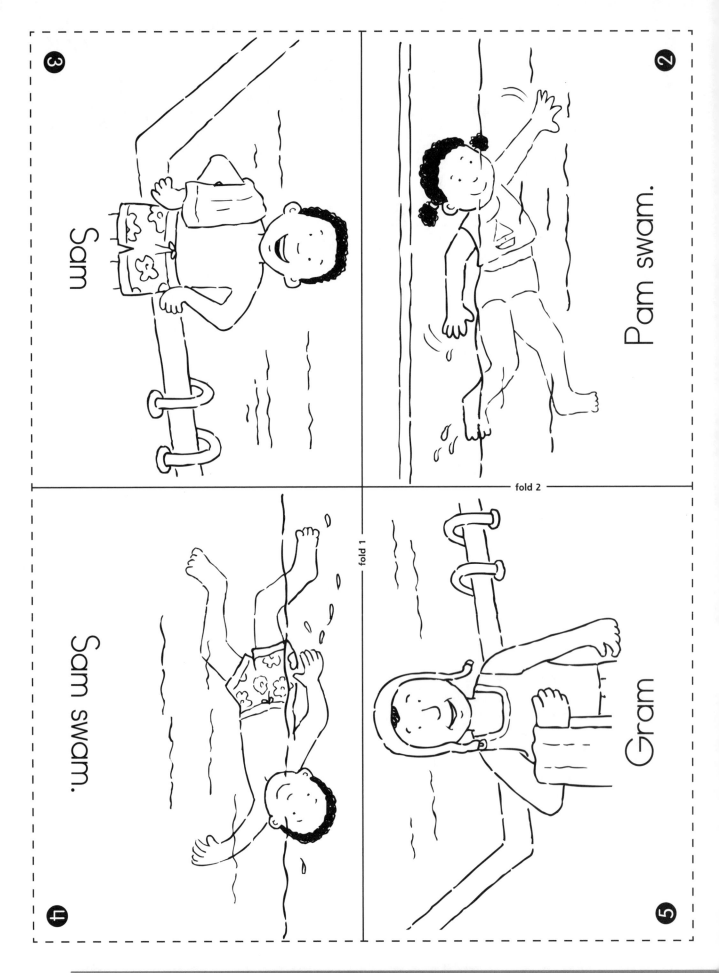

❸

Sam

❷

Pam swam.

fold 2

fold 1

Gram

Sam swam.

❹

❺

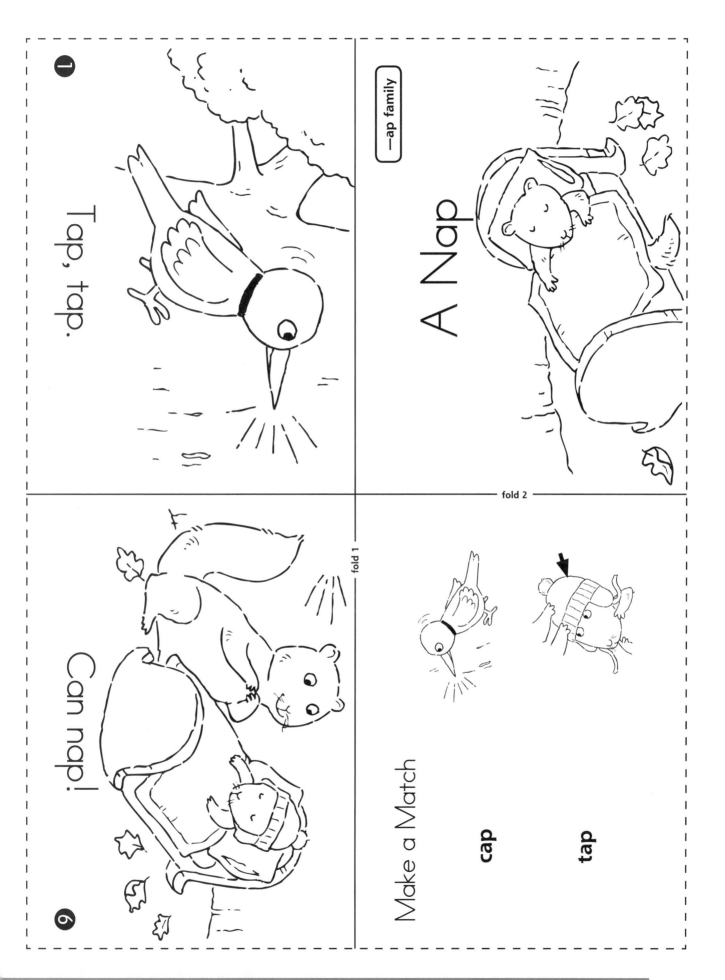

**1**

Tap, tap.

—ap family

A Nap

fold 2

fold 1

Can nap!

**6**

Make a Match

cap

tap

③ Tap, tap, tap.

② Can't nap!

tap
tap

④ Add a nap cap.

⑤ Tap, tap, tap.

fold 2

fold 1

Basic Phonics Skills, Level B • EMC 3319 • ©2004 by Evan-Moor Corp.

**1**

Sit, sit.

Fit It!

**6**

It fit! It fit!

Make a Match

sit

fit

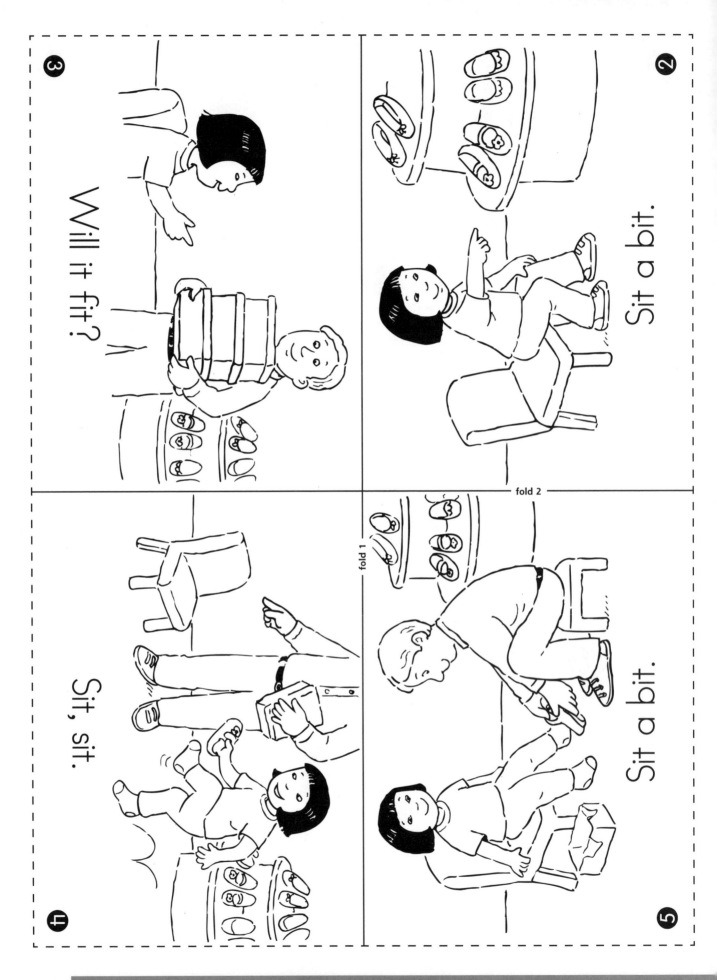

③ Will it fit?

② Sit a bit.

④ Sit, sit.

⑤ Sit a bit.

**1**

It is a big rig.

**—ig family**

The Big Dig

fold 2

fold 1

It is a BIG dig!

**6**

Make a Match

rig

dig

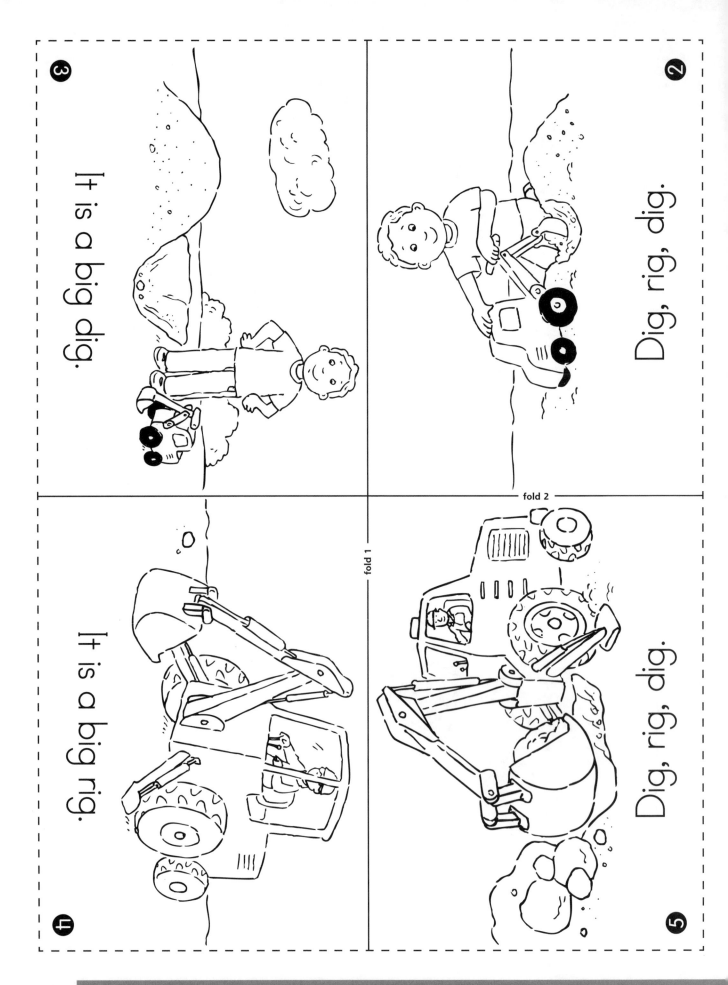

**3** It is a big dig.

**2** Dig, rig, dig.

**4** It is a big rig.

**5** Dig, rig, dig.

fold 2

fold 1

 Basic Phonics Skills, Level B • EMC 3319 • ©2004 by Evan-Moor Corp.

1

Tad

—ad family

# Tad and Dad

fold 2

fold 1

Glad Tad and Dad

6

Make a Match

sad

glad

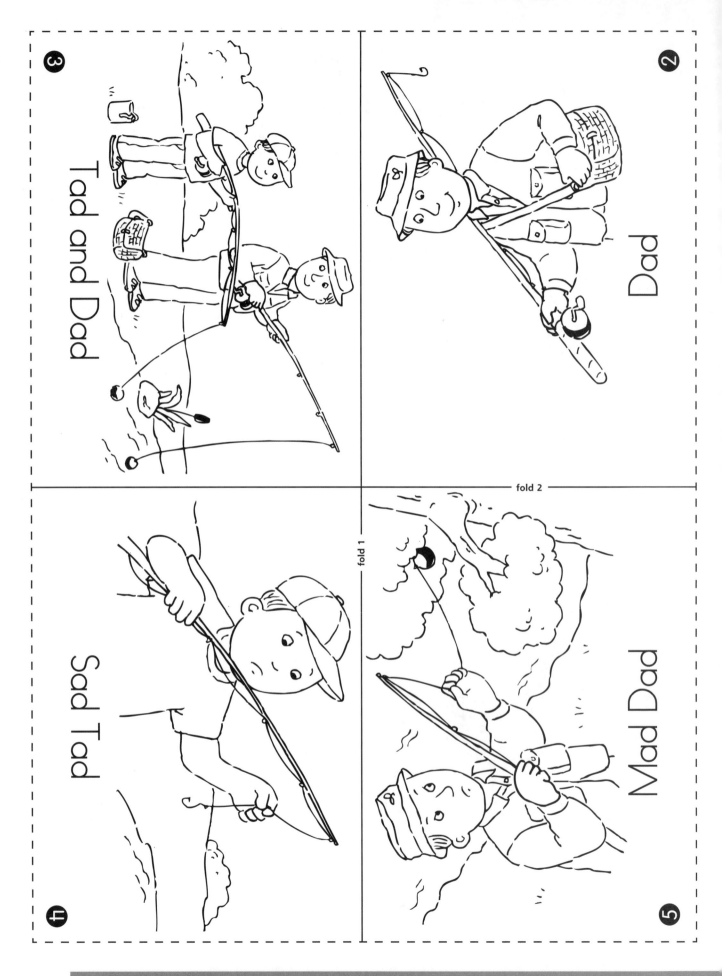

**3** Tad and Dad

**2** Dad

**4** Sad Tad

**5** Mad Dad

fold 1

fold 2

Basic Phonics Skills, Level B • EMC 3319 • ©2004 by Evan-Moor Corp.

—at family

At Bat

**1** a bat

**6** Matt at bat.

Make a Match

Pat

Matt

**3**

Pat at bat.

**2**

a hat

Pat

fold 2

fold 1

**4**

a bat

**5**

a hat

Matt

Basic Phonics Skills, Level B • EMC 3319 • ©2004 by Evan-Moor Corp.

**1**

Jack

—ack family

# Jack's Pack

*fold 2*

*fold 1*

Jack's backpack

**6**

Make a Match

**yak**

**snack**

**tack**

❸ Pack a sack.

❷ Pack a snack.

❹ Pack a tack.

❺ Pack a yak.

fold 2

fold 1

 Basic Phonics Skills, Level B • EMC 3319 • ©2004 by Evan-Moor Corp.

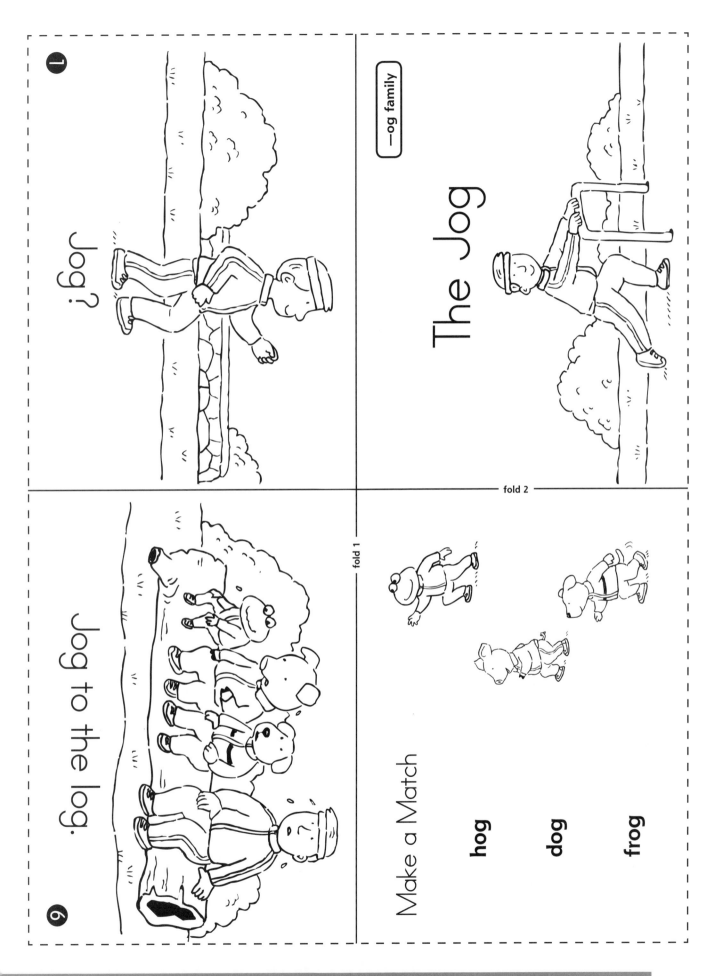

**1**

Jog?

The Jog

fold 2

fold 1

Make a Match

**hog**

**dog**

**frog**

Jog to the log.

**6**

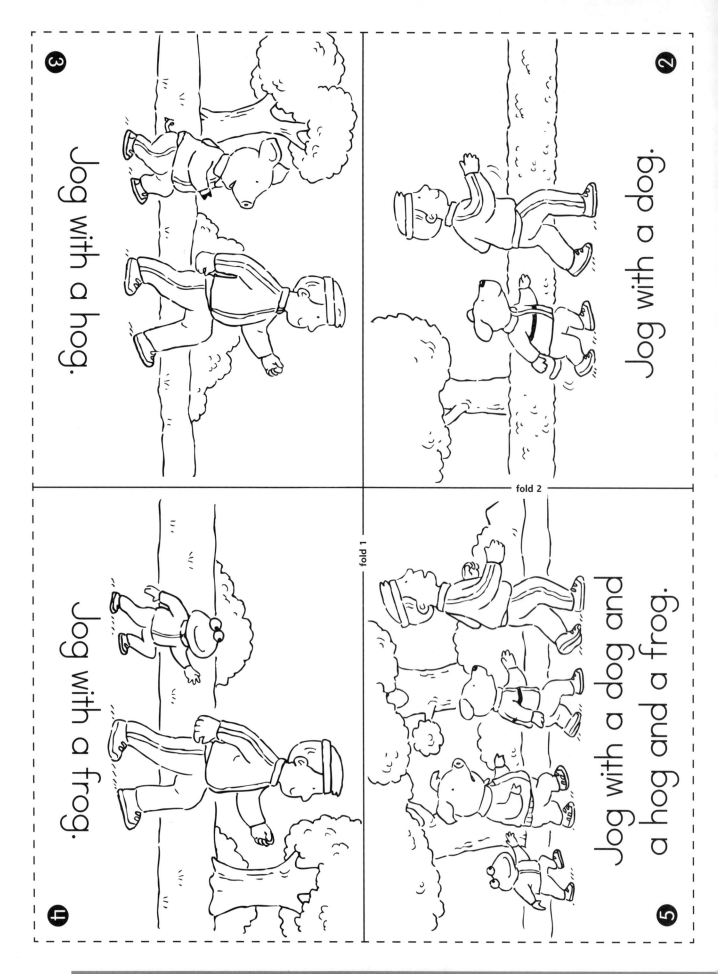

**3** Jog with a hog.

**2** Jog with a dog.

**4** Jog with a frog.

**5** Jog with a dog and a hog and a frog.

fold 2

fold 1

**Little Phonics Readers**

Basic Phonics Skills, Level B • EMC 3319 • ©2004 by Evan-Moor Corp.

**1**

Nan

**6**

the clan

—an family

# Company's Coming

fold 2

fold 1

Make a Match

pan

can

fan

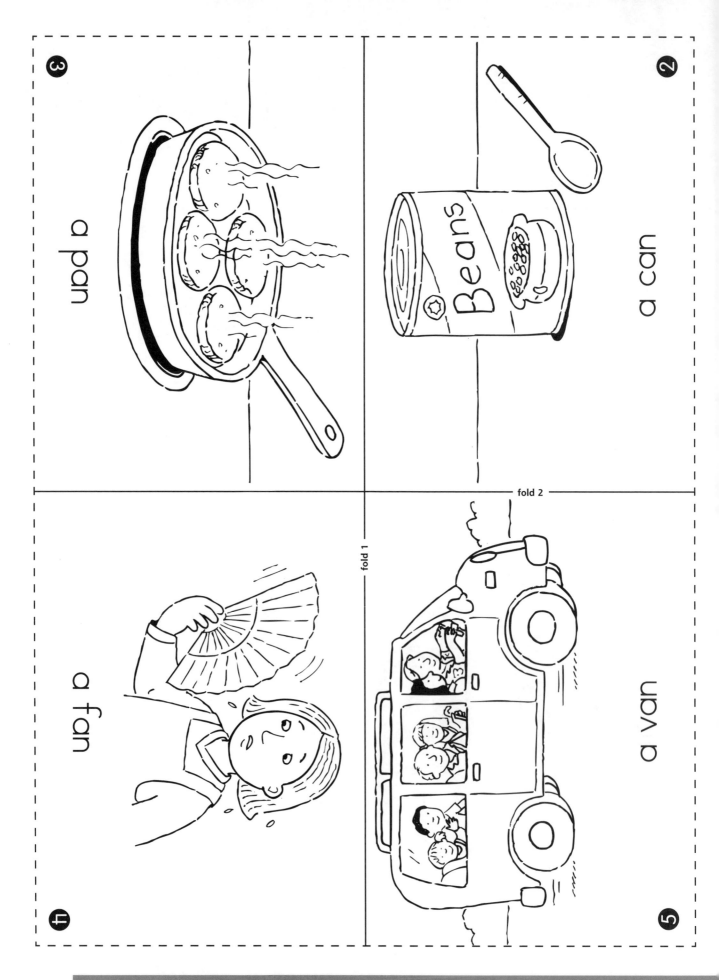

❸

a pan

❷

a can

❹

a fan

❺

a van

fold 2

fold 1

Basic Phonics Skills, Level B • EMC 3319 • ©2004 by Evan-Moor Corp.

**1**

I pick.

—ick family

A Trick

fold 2

fold 1

Do the trick.

**6**

Make a Match

**Dick**

**Nick**

**stick**

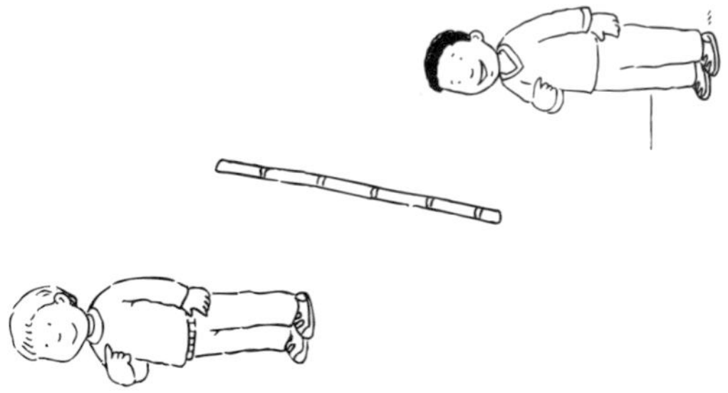

③

I pick.

②

I pick Nick.

fold 2

fold 1

Pick a stick.

④

I pick Dick.

⑤

# Answer Key

**Page 8**   Circled: bee, barn, box

**Page 9**   **b**ook, **b**ug, **b**ell, **b**one

**Page 10**  sub, crab, bib

**Page 11**  1. su**b**; 4. ri**b**; 5. cri**b**; 6. tu**b**

**Page 12**  1. **b**ird; 2. ri**b**; 3. cra**b**; 4. **b**ed; 5. **b**ike; 6. cri**b**; 7. **b**ook; 8. tu**b**

**Page 13**  1. **b**us; 2. **b**at; 3. tu**b**; 4. **b**ug; 5. cra**b**; 6. **b**ib, bi**b**

**Page 14**  Circled: seal, soup, sandwich, salt

**Page 15**  **s**oap, **s**eal, **s**un, **s**ix, **s**ock

**Page 16**  nuts, walrus, octopus

**Page 17**  1. ga**s**; 3. bu**s**; 4. ye**s**

**Page 18**  1. dre**ss**; 2. gra**ss**; 3. ki**ss**; 5. gla**ss**

**Page 19**  **Sub:** sun, saw; **Bus:** gas, glass

**Page 20**  1. **s**un; 2. **s**ub; 3. gra**ss**; 4. **s**oup; 5. **s**aw; 6. dre**ss**

**Page 21**  Circled: milk, moon, mouse, mask

**Page 22**  1. **m**an; 2. **m**ap; 4. **m**op; 5. **m**oon; 6. **m**ug

**Page 23**  Circled: ram, broom, drum

**Page 24**  1. ar**m**; 3. dru**m**; 4. ja**m**; 5. plu**m**; 7. ha**m**; 8. far**m**

**Page 25**  1. **m**ask; 2. **m**itten; 3. wor**m**; 4. **m**irror; 5. plu**m**; 6. broo**m**

**Page 26**  1. **m**oon; 2. **m**ug; 3. gu**m**; 4. cla**m**; 5. ha**m**; 6. dru**m**

**Page 27**  1. map (m); 2. bike (b); 3. balloon (b); 4. mitten (m); 5. basket (b); 6. soap (s); 7. sock (s); 8. moon (m); 9. seven (s)

**Page 28**  1. **m**ug; 2. **s**aw; 3. **b**ook; 4. **s**un; 5. **b**ell; 6. **m**oon; 7. **b**ed; 8. **m**op; 9. **s**eal

**Page 29**  1. drum (m); 2. crab (b); 3. bus (s); 4. ham (m); 5. sub (b); 6. broom (m); 7. tub (b); 8. gas (s); 9. octopus (s)

**Page 30**  1. broom (m); 2. grass (s); 3. rib (b); 4. octopus (s); 5. bib (b); 6. plum (m); 7. crib (b); 8. clam (m); 9. kiss (s)

**Page 31**  Circled: turkey, two, telephone, tire

**Page 32**  1. **t**op; 2. **t**ape; 3. **t**en; 5. **t**ie; 6. **t**ub

**Page 33**  hat, nut, cat, net

©2004 by Evan-Moor Corp. • Basic Phonics Skills, Level B • EMC 3319

**Page 34** 1. bat; 2. foot; 4. coat; 5. boot; 6. hat; 8. cat

**Page 35** 1. top; 2. boat; 3. tire; 4. robot; 5. rocket; 6. tub

**Page 36** 1. top; 2. boat; 3. cat; 4. tag; 5. jet; 6. goat

**Page 37** Circled: fish, five, foot, fan, fork

**Page 38** 1. fish-fish; 2. fan-fan; 3. fox-fox; 4. five-five

**Page 39** wolf, elf, scarf

**Page 40** 1. wolf; 2. leaf; 4. hoof; 5. elf

**Page 41** 1. off; 3. cuff; 4. cliff; 6. puff

**Page 42 Fox:** fan, fish, fire; **Wolf:** chef, leaf, scarf

**Page 43** 1. fork-chef; 2. foot-football; 3. wolf-fox

**Page 44** Circled: kangaroo, kitten, key, king

**Page 45** 1. cat; 2. key; 3. kite; 4. cow; 5. king; 6. coat

**Page 46** sock, hook, truck, duck

**Page 47 Key:** kitten, king; **Sack:** fork, sock, block, rake

**Page 48** 1. clock; 2. desk; 3. stick; 4. book; 5. sock; 6. sack; 7. hook; 8. lock

**Page 49** 1. king; 2. stick; 3. lock; 4. kite; 5. kitten; 6. sock; 7. duck; 8. book; 9. hook

**Page 50** 1. fish (f); 2. king (k); 3. tooth (t); 4. tent (t); 5. tape (t); 6. five (f); 7. fan (f); 8. key (k); 9. fork (f)

**Page 51** 1. kite (k); 2. feather (f); 3. tire (t); 4. five (f); 5. kangaroo (k); 6. fence (f); 7. turtle (t); 8. ten (t); 9. foot (f)

**Page 52** 1. brick (k); 2. chef (f); 3. cat (t); 4. leaf (f); 5. foot (t); 6. sock (k); 7. book (k); 8. duck (k); 9. scarf (f)

**Page 53** 1. truck (k); 2. elf (f); 3. boat (t); 4. wolf (f); 5. boot (t); 6. lock (k); 7. coat (t); 8. sack (k); 9. roof (f)

**Page 54** Colored: pan, pillow, pencil, popcorn, pig

**Page 55** 1. pin; 2. pup; 3. pie; 5. pig; 6. pear

**Page 56 Pig:** pin, pie, pencil, pickle; **Sheep:** cup, drip

**Page 57** 1. cap; 2. jeep; 4. sheep; 6. map

**Page 58** 1. mop; 2. pickle; 3. pig; 4. soap; 5. jeep; 6. paint; 7. top; 8. sheep; 9. pen

**Page 59** 1. pot; 2. map; 3. pig; 4. pup; 5. pail; 6. top

**Page 60** Circled: rug, rope, rabbit, ring, rake

Basic Phonics Skills, Level B • EMC 3319 • ©2004 by Evan-Moor Corp.

**Page 61** 1. **r**ock; 2. **r**at; 3. **r**ing; 5. **r**oof; 6. **r**abbit

**Page 62** Colored: car, bear, ear, deer, chair

**Page 63** 1. pea**r**; 2. dee**r**; 3. doo**r**; 5. fou**r**; 6. ca**r**

**Page 64 Rug:** rattle, roof, rat, ring; **Chair:** star, four, guitar, bear

**Page 65** 1. ear; 2. car; 3. door; 4. rake; 5. **r**am; 6. ja**r**

**Page 66** Circled: vine, vase, violin, van

**Page 67** **v**an, **v**est, **v**ase, **v**ine

**Page 68 Vase:** vacuum, van, vegetables, violin; **Glove:** hive, five, sleeve, stove

**Page 69 Valley:** violin, vacuum, vet; **Cave:** stove, sleeve, wave

**Page 70** 1. vine; 2. **v**an; 3. wave; 4. **v**est; 5. hi**v**e; 6. **v**ase

**Page 71** 1. pencil (p); 2. rose (r); 3. van (v); 4. rake (r); 5. violin (v); 6. piano (p); 7. vest (v); 8. pillow (p); 9. rabbit (r)

**Page 72** 1. pizza (p); 2. ring (r); 3. valentine (v); 4. robot (r); 5. vase (v); 6. pan (p); 7. vine (v); 8. parachute (p); 9. rope (r)

**Page 73** 1. cup (p); 2. star (r); 3. glove (v); 4. bear (r); 5. five (v); 6. mop (p); 7. sleeve (v); 8. lip (p); 9. car (r)

**Page 74** 1. door (r); 2. rope (p); 3. jar (r); 4. soap (p); 5. mop (p); 6. hive (v); 7. five (v); 8. cave (v); 9. cap (p); 10. sheep (p); 11. four (r); 12. cup (p)

**Page 75** Circled: doll, dinosaur, dollar, duck

**Page 76** 1. **d**og; 3. **d**ime; 4. **d**esk

**Page 77** Colored: seed, hand, sled, braid, bread

**Page 78** 1. be**d**; 2. li**d**; 3. mu**d**; 4. toa**d**; 6. sle**d**; 9. bir**d**

**Page 79 Duck:** doll, doctor, dime; **Pond:** lid, sled, bird

**Page 80** 1. **d**og; 2. **d**esk; 3. see**d**; 4. **d**eer; 5. sle**d**; 6. bea**d**; 7. **d**ish; 8. toa**d**; 9. **d**ime

**Page 81** Circled: house, hat, hand, hook, hoe

**Page 82 Inside the heart:** hen, hippo, house, hat; **Outside the heart:** king, cup

**Page 83** 1. **h**ive-**h**oney; 2. **h**orse-**h**ay; 3. **h**en-**h**atch; 4. **h**at-**h**ead

**Page 84** 1. **h**oe; 2. **h**at; 3. **h**ook; 4. **h**en; 5. **h**orn; 6. **h**ose

**Page 85** Circled: gate, girl, goose, gum, ghost

**Page 86** 1. **g**old; 2. **g**um; 3. **g**ate; 4. **g**oat; 5. **g**irl

**Page 87** goose, goat, gum, guitar

**Page 88** 1. pig; 2. leg; 4. flag; 5. log; 6. wig

**Page 89 Goose:** gift, gas, goat; **Egg:** rug, wig, dog

**Page 90** 1. goose; 2. dog; 3. frog; 4. pig; 5. goat; 6. bug

**Page 91** 1. desk (d); 2. heart (h); 3. gate (g); 4. hose (h); 5. goose (g); 6. dog (d); 7. goat (g); 8. duck (d); 9. hat (h)

**Page 92** 1. guitar (g); 2. horse (h); 3. doll (d); 4. hat (h); 5. door (d); 6. gum (g); 7. deer (d); 8. hammer (h); 9. girl (g)

**Page 93** 1. bed-sled; 2. egg-flag; 3. bug-dog; 4. sled-bird; 5. dog-pig

**Page 94** Circled: lamp, leg, log, lunchbox, lip

**Page 95** 1. lamp; 2. leaf; 3. lock; 5. lion; 6. ladder

**Page 96** doll, bell, school, nail

**Page 97** 1. pool; 2. bowl; 3. wheel; 5. heel; 6. seal

**Page 98 Lake:** ladder, leaf, lamp, lemon; **Pool:** nail, hill, bell, tail

**Page 99** 1. lion; 2. seal; 3. eel; 4. owl; 5. lizard; 6. camel

**Page 100** 1. frog-bug; 2. snail-bell; 3. dog-pig; 4. nail-doll; 5. bowl-pool

**Page 101** Circled: jeep, jacks, jet, jar, jelly beans

**Page 102** jam, jar, jeep, jug, jet

**Page 103** juice, jam, jaw, jump

**Page 104 Jump rope**–jar, jet; **George Washington**–giant, giraffe; **Goat**–gum

**Page 105 G**–giant, gems, giraffe; **J**–jam, jacks, jet

**Page 106** 1. bridge-cage; 2. badge-fudge; 3. garage-orange; jam, jeans, jeep

**Page 107** Circled: nail, newspaper, nine, nut

**Page 108** 1. neck; 3. nut; 4. net; 5. note

**Page 109** button, can, moon, bean

**Page 110** 1. train; 3. wagon; 4. van; 6. lion

**Page 111** 1. lemon; 2. nurse; 3. nail; 4. fan; 5. nose; 6. spoon

**Page 112** 1. pen; 2. nickel; 3. nest; 4. can; 5. train; 6. nut

**Page 113** 1. lemon (l); 2. jar (j); 3. nest (n); 4. jet (j); 5. nickel (n); 6. lion (l); 7. nail (n); 8. lamp (l); 9. jump rope (j)

**Page 114** 1. jet-jar; 2. juice-jet; 3. nurse-nail; 4. lion-lock

     Basic Phonics Skills, Level B • EMC 3319 • ©2004 by Evan-Moor Corp.

**Page 115** 1. shell (l); 2. queen (n); 3. moon (n); 4. doll (l); 5. fan (n); 6. wagon (n); 7. nail (l); 8. ball (l); 9. can (n)

**Page 116** 1. pen (n); 2. pail (l); 3. pan (n); 4. owl (l); 5. eel (l); 6. ten (n); 7. van (n); 8. nail (l); 9. snail (l)

**Page 117** Circled: watch, worm, wig, web

**Page 118** 1. **w**asp; 2. **w**ig; 3. **w**ell; 4. **w**olf; 6. **w**ood

**Page 119** 1. pig-wig; 2. cave-wave; 3. ball-wall; 4. sing-wing; 5. net-wet

**Page 120** Circled: yak, yolk, yawn, yarn

**Page 121** 1. **y**arn; 3. **y**awn; 4. **y**o-yo; 5. **y**ak

**Page 122** 1. barn-yarn; 2. lawn-yawn; 3. jam-yam; 4. card-yard; Pictures should reflect the new words.

**Page 123** Circled: queen, quarter, question mark, quail

**Page 124** 1. pail-quail; 2. tack-quack; 3. teen-queen; 4. tick-quick; Pictures should reflect the new words.

**Page 125** 1. **qu**ack; 2. **qu**iet; 3. **qu**ill; 4. **qu**iz

**Page 126** Circled: zipper, zero, zoo

**Page 127** 1. **z**ebra; 2. **z**ero; 3. **z**ipper; 5. **z**oo; 6. **z**igzag

**Page 128** 1. **z**ero; 3. **z**ipper; 4. **z**ebra; 6. **z**igzag

**Page 129** 1. fu**zz**; 2. bree**z**e; 3. bu**zz**; 4. pri**z**e; 5. qui**z**; 6. fi**zz**

**Page 130** 1. rose (right); 2. zebra (left); 3. zero (left); 4. eyes (right); 5. nose (right); 6. hose (right)

**Page 131** 1. bree**z**e; 2. bu**zz**; 3. ro**s**e; 4. tree**s**; 5. **z**oom; 6. **z**oo

**Page 132** 1. no; 2. no; 3. yes; 4. yes; 5. no; 6. yes

**Page 133** ax, box, fox, six

**Page 134** 1. bo**x**; 2. si**x**; 3. **X** ray; 5. fo**x**

**Page 135** 1. ta**x**; 2. fi**x**; 3. sa**x**; 4. si**x**; 5. tu**x**; 6. bo**x**

**Page 136** 1. quilt (qu); 2. window (w); 3. yarn (y); 4. queen (qu); 5. zebra (z); 6. X ray (x); 7. web (w); 8. yo-yo (y); 9. zipper (z)

**Page 137** 1. wig (w); 2. wagon (w); 3. yak (y); 4. quail (qu); 5. zebra (z); 6. X ray (x); 7. yo-yo (y); 8. quarter (qu); 9. zero (z)

**Page 138** 1. mix (x); 2. sneeze (z); 3. box (x); 4. prize (z); 5. fox (x); 6. fuzz (z); 7. six (x); 8. ax (x); 9. ox (x)

**Page 140** Red: a, e, i, o, u; All others blue

**Page 141** Circled: cap, rat, map, bat,

**Page 142** 1. map-map; 2. bat-bat; 3. fan-fan; 4. bag-bag; 5. hat-hat

**Page 143** 1. cat; 2. ham; 3. map; 4. van; 5. jam

**Page 144** 1. cab; 2. bat; 3. bag; 4. fan; 5. hat

**Page 145** 1. cap; 2. tag; 3. rat; 4. ram; 5. man; 6. pan

**Page 146** 1. can; 2. bag; 3. hat; 4. fan; 5. bat; 6. tag

**Page 147** 1. Dad had a **nap**; 2. The **cat** ran fast; 3. Nan is **sad**; 4. Jack has a **bag**.

**Page 148** 1. Ann ran by a can; 2. Jan has a ham; 3. Max is mad at Jan; 4. Ann can pat the cat.

**Page 149**

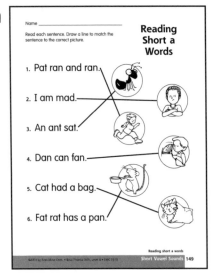

**Page 150** jam, bag, pan, cap

**Page 151** 1. can; 2. bag; 3. jam; 4. sad; 5. pan; 6. hat; 7. cat; 8. van; 9. map

**Page 152** wig, pin, bib, six, sticks

**Page 153**

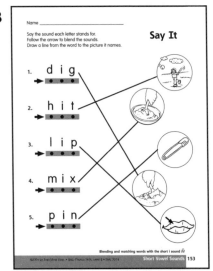

**Page 154** 1. bib; 2. fin; 3. lid; 4. hit; 5. six

**Page 155** 1. wig; 2. rib; 3. rip; 4. pig; 5. bib

**Page 156** 1. zip; 2. six; 3. fin; 4. lid; 5. pin; 6. wig

**Page 157** 1. pig; 2. pin; 3. six; 4. lip; 5. wig; 6. fin

**Page 158** 1. It is a big **pig**; 2. Liz can **hit** it; 3. It did not **fit**; 4. Liz likes to **sit**.

**Page 159** 1. Tim can hit; 2. Sis has a bib; 3. The pig can win; 4. Vic can dig a pit.

**Page 160**

**Page 161 Pig:** lid, wig, 6, bib; **Cat:** fan, pan, hand, rat

**Page 162** 1. lid; 2. pig; 3. wig; 4. lip; 5. bib; 6. rib; 7. pin; 8. fin; 9. six

**Page 163** 1. cat; 2. bag; 3. six; 4. rip; 5. van; 6. lip; 7. wig; 8. pan; 9. pin

**Page 164** Circled: pot, cot, mop, dot

**Page 165** 1. top-top; 2. rod-rod; 3. pot-pot; 4. box-box; 5. dot-dot

**Page 166** 1. mop; 2. hot; 3. box; 4. cot; 5. cob

**Page 167** 1. dog; 2. dot; 3. hot; 4. rod; 5. top

**Page 168** 1. log; 2. mop; 3. pot; 4. cob; 5. fox; 6. hot

**Page 169** 1. mop; 2. top; 3. cot; 4. dot; 5. pot; 6. box

**Page 170** 1. Tom got a **box**; 2. The lid is on the **pot**; 3. A **fox** is on a log; 4. The hog has a **cob**.

**Page 171** 1. Did Don lock it?; 2. Is Mom hot?; 3. Is the dot on top?; 4. Is the dog in the fog?

**Page 172**

**Page 173 Fox:** hop, mop, frog, top; **Pig:** lip, pin, hit, fin

**Page 174** 1. pod; 2. log; 3. mop; 4. cob; 5. pot; 6. hog; 7. dot; 8. fox; 9. cot

**Page 175** 1. top; 2. lid; 3. bat; 4. fox; 5. ham; 6. bib; 7. pot; 8. six; 9. fan

**Page 176** Circled: jet, bed, web, sled

**Page 177** 1. egg-egg; 2. men-men; 3. web-web; 4. hen-hen; 5. wet-wet

**Page 178** 1. bed; 2. jet; 3. pen; 4. web; 5. ten

**Page 179** 1. men; 2. vet; 3. pen; 4. wet; 5. web

**Page 180** 1. hen; 2. egg; 3. leg; 4. jet; 5. wet; 6. vet

**Page 181** 1. men; 2. leg; 3. jet; 4. bed; 5. vet; 6. ten

**Page 182** 1. Ben is on the **bed**; 2. Yes, Jen is **wet**; 3. My pet can **beg**; 4. The hen is in the **pen**.

**Page 183** 1. Ken has a net; 2. The men met by a jet; 3. Jen has a pet hen; 4. My leg is wet.

**Page 184**

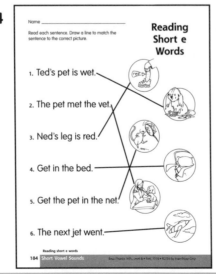

Basic Phonics Skills, Level B • EMC 3319 • ©2004 by Evan-Moor Corp.

**Page 185** **Jet:** leg, web, ten, men; **Hot dog:** lock, top, log, stop

**Page 186** 1. pet; 2. pen; 3. web; 4. bed; 5. net; 6. jet; 7. leg; 8. ten; 9. vet

**Page 187** 1. hat; 2. bed; 3. pin; 4. cat; 5. map; 6. leg; 7. man; 8. dog; 9. jet

**Page 188** Circled: cup, drum, rug, gum

**Page 189** 1. mug-mug; 2. cut-cut; 3. rug-rug; 4. bun-bun; 5. jug-jug

**Page 190** 1. bug; 2. cup; 3. tub; 4. bus; 5. pup

**Page 191** 1. mug; 2. nut; 3. tub; 4. gum; 5. sub

**Page 192** 1. cub; 2. run; 3. hug; 4. rug; 5. bug; 6. sun

**Page 193** 1. hut; 2. bug; 3. cup; 4. bun; 5. tub; 6. sub

**Page 194** 1. You must not **hug** a skunk; 2. Bud gets on the **bus**; 3. The mud is on the **pup**; 4. I hung the **rug** in the sun.

**Page 195** 1. The bug is in a cup; 2. The sun is up; 3. The cub dug up a nut; 4. Bud cut up the rug.

**Page 196**

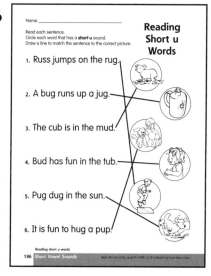

**Page 197** **Sun:** rug, gum, tub, mug; **Hens:** bed, pen, ten, fence

**Page 198** 1. tub; 2. mug; 3.cub; 4. pup; 5. sun; 6. sub; 7. nut; 8. hut; 9. gum

**Page 199** 1. map; 2. hen; 3. pig; 4. log; 5. bus; 6. jet; 7. lip; 8. top; 9. cup

**Page 200** 1. pan, hat; 2. bed, net; 3. lid, bib; 4. dog, box; 5. bug, cup

**Page 202** 1. bed**s**; 2. hat**s**; 3. pin**s**; 4. nut**s**; 5. sub**s**

**Page 203** 1. six**es**; 2. dress**es**; 3. dish**es**; 4. box**es**; 5. bus**es**; 6. kiss**es**

**Page 204** 1. pen**s**; 2. ax**es**; 3. log**s**; 4. can**s**; 5. bush**es**; 6. bus**es**

**Page 205** 1. bats; 2. buses; 3. cans; 4. boxes; 5. dresses; 6. bushes

**Page 206** 1. My **cat** is in its bed; 2. The **dishes** are by the pan; 3. Linn has lots of **eggs**; 4. Here is a **jug** for you; 5. Mom gave me a **kiss**.

**Page 207** 1. ball; 2. wish; 3. pass; 4. hit; 5. bus

**Page 208** jumped, jumping; climbed, climbing; looked, looking; played, playing; walked, walking; washed, washing

**Page 209** 1. The bee **buzzed** by my ear; 2. Nan is **helping** her dad; 3. Max **tossed** the ball to Jan; 4. Kim is **jumping** over the box.

**Page 210** 1. box̲es; 2. spill̲ed; 3. duck̲s; 4. dress̲es; 5. brush̲ing; 6. nail̲s

**Page 214** 1. h**im**, 2. dr**um**, 3. cl**am**, 4. j**am**, 5. g**um**, 6. sw**im**

**Page 215** 1. rim; 2. dim; 3. ram; 4. ham; 5. plum; 6. yum; New word answers will vary, but must include the *am*, *im*, or *um* word family.

**Page 217** 1. l**ip**; 2. m**op**; 3. c**ap**; 4. cl**ap**; 5. z**ip**; 6. st**op**

**Page 218** 1. s**ip**; 2. h**op**; 3. m**ap**; 4. dr**ip**; 5. n**ap**; 6. t**op**; New word answers will vary, but must include the *ip*, *ap*, or *op* word family.

**Page 220** 1. b**at**, 2. h**it**, 3. j**et**, 4. h**at**, 5. n**et**, 6. s**it**

**Page 221** 1. cat; 2. wet; 3. slit; 4. vet; 5. flat; 6. flit; New word answers will vary, but must include the *at*, *et*, or *it* word family.

**Page 223** 1. d**ad**; 2. sl**ed**; 3. r**od**; 4. s**ad**; 5. n**od**; 6. b**ed**

**Page 224** 1. mad; 2. pod; 3. wed; 4. glad; 5. fled; 6. cod; New word answers will vary, but must include the *ad*, *ed*, or *od* word family.

**Page 226** 1. c**an**; 2. s**un**; 3. p**in**; 4. r**an**; 5. w**in**; 6. b**un**

**Page 227** 1. fan; 2. fin; 3. sun; 4. twin; 5. man; 6. spun; New word answers will vary, but must include the *an*, *in*, or *un* word family.

**Page 229** 1. p**ig**; 2. l**og**; 3. d**og**; 4. m**ug**; 5. w**ig**; 6. r**ug**

**Page 230** 1. big; 2. bug; 3. dog; 4. twig; 5. frog; 6. hug; New word answers will vary, but must include the *ig*, *og*, or *ug* word family.

**Page 232** 1. s**ack**; 2. t**ick**; 3. n**eck**; 4. s**ick**; 5. cr**ack**; 6. sp**eck**

**Page 233** 1. quack; 2. peck; 3. neck; 4. kick; 5. black; 6. stick; New word answers will vary, but must include the *ack*, *eck*, or *ick* word family.

**Page 234** 1. cat; 2. dog; 3. sack; 4. lick; 5. hop; 6. fan; 7. run; 8. bed; 9. hit; New word answers will vary, but must be spelled correctly.

Basic Phonics Skills, Level B • EMC 3319 • ©2004 by Evan-Moor Corp.